Everyday Heroes 2

Another Collection of Inspirational & Motivational

Stories From Around the World

COMPILED BY MATT BACAK

ISBN-13: 978-0997224047

DEDICATION

Dedicated to all the Heroes out there, doing their part every day...
Including this book's charity, the Cancer Research Institute.

TABLE OF CONTENTS

ACKNOWLEDGMENTS

Thank you to all the authors who shared their stories in this book,
and a special thank you to the team who pulled it all together…
Jeanne Kolenda, Leon Kolenda, Sean McCarthy, and my wife, Stephanie.

THE BUTTERFLY EFFECT

ANDREW GUNN

Once upon a time, there was a little boy who lived an ordinary and unremarkable life. Like most 10-year-old boys he just whiled away the days dreaming of adventure. Although he could barely read and write, every week he visited the library to browse through the heavy picture books. The images inside fired his vivid imagination. It was easier and more fun than trying to read the words.

Then one day he discovered a giant book about the Golden Age of Hollywood. But this was no ordinary book. This book was about the people behind the camera – the producers, the cinematographers, and screenwriters. And in that moment that little boy's life became extra-ordinary. He had discovered something that would become a lifelong obsession. He had discovered *filmmaking*. But more compelling was the discovery of the role of the DIRECTOR, the person who directs and influences all the creative, technical and artistic elements to convey the vision and story to the audience. It was an epiphany.

I Was a Brainless 10-Year-Old Boy…

…when I decided that one day I was going to be a film director. I wasn't very bright and had a terrible time at school. At age 12, I required special workbooks and remedial classes in reading and writing. I was partially illiterate and images and films became my access to stories and storytelling. I was a young boy with a big imagination and sky-high dreams and a shameful lack of confidence and self-esteem. Later I would often think that my aspirations and expectations severely outweighed my capabilities and talents. But I didn't give up. I just kept on moving in the direction of my 'dream'.

Fast-forward 25 years to the 90's and the senseless dreamer had become a multi-award-winning director and screenwriter. But to reach this level of accomplishment took many years of persistence, practice, sacrifice, commitment, self-education and good old-fashioned blood, sweat and tears.

By this time, I was also a proud father of two beautiful and bright children, with a mortgage, bills, two cars and a cat. I'd been previously married, had an affair, been divorced, and suffered an incapacitating spinal injury, which resulted in emergency surgery. I was in agony for two years.

Truthfully, between 1993 and 1999, I was a mess. My life was a mess. All self-inflicted. I was mainly out of work, in a relationship that hadn't started on the best footing. I was frustrated, depressed, resentful and in constant pain. My partner had to put up with a lot as I dealt with my *negative shit* - guilt, anxiety and desperation. I was so stressed out I was suffering from debilitating panic attacks, too.

My son was born in 1999 and my daughter in 2002, and becoming a father gave me a sharp kick in the ass, and a giant slap across the face. If there's anything I'm most proud of and grateful for, it's being a dad to two beautiful, bright, healthy, and genuinely amazing souls.

To cut a long story short, I finally started to pick up work as a professional director, at first directing comedy and children's drama. And in 2006, I got my BIG BREAK and was invited to direct what I considered at the time to be the coolest drama on British TV, the BAFTA award-winning *Life On Mars*. Everything changed on the day I received the call from my agent. All the years of hard work, struggle and persistence had finally paid off. I had become a *top director*. This was A-list stuff, happening to me. And about time!

Little did I know that (for me, at least) success was going to be surprisingly and disappointingly ephemeral.

From The Sublime To The Ridiculous

Between 2006 and 2011 I was on an ascending star, going from one contract to another, directing popular high-end drama for prime time TV. I just worked and worked and worked, excited and proud to have 'made it'. I felt *successful* for the first time in my life, in every way.

I gradually discovered, however, that my career was not conducive to a balanced home life or relationship. I was always away from home, working 80+ hours per week, leaving my family to fend for themselves. And financially it was either feast or famine.

The work lifestyle was far from 'glamorous'. The relentless schedules, missed holidays, missed family time, unsocial hours and constant commuting gradually took their toll.

By 2012 everything had changed. After a couple of awfully unpleasant experiences with some 'executive producers' (a.k.a my bosses), my career took a rapid nosedive. The punitive nature of the post-production process (that's the editing and assembling of the film), became like an inquisition, and I was the accused. As a director you can be singled out, often blamed for script and story errors, and even threatened and intimidated. You are routinely disrespected. One male producer even *bullied* me on a frequent basis, but I wasn't aware it was 'workplace bullying' until a colleague pointed it out.

Quite frankly, by this time I had fallen out of love with my work. I knew something was wrong because I lived in dread of making the 'wrong' decision on set. I was suspicious and secretly nervous of the producers and executives, and it just wasn't fun anymore. It had become abundantly clear to me that on many levels there is very little respect for UK drama directors, or even an appreciation of just how bloody hard and challenging the task is in these days of increasingly ambitious production values, tighter schedules, shamefully late scripts and squeezed budgets.

The hideous politics of the industry finally came at me like a towering tsunami. I was powerless. It was a calamity I couldn't avoid. I know for a fact that the 'incidents' with the producers and my faltering career were not unconnected. I know for a fact that the 'bully producer' had bad-mouthed me to another producer who was keen to hire me, and the job abruptly went away. Suddenly I couldn't get arrested. The interviews diminished, the offers stopped.

From there on things dismantled very rapidly. It was now 2013 and within just a few short months I was struggling to pay the mortgage and the bills. Something I never expected to happen, happened. We collided head-on with a reinforced concrete wall known as *financial difficulty* - bankruptcy. It happened so quickly it took my breath away. So bad was it that my relationship with my partner, the mother of my children, began to disassemble. The cracks that were already there broke apart. Financial difficulty can be the destroyer of even the strongest relationship. Ours wasn't strong enough. She 'ran-for-the-hills' in panic (I don't blame her), and I was left to deal with the fallout.

Our converted barn in the beautiful English countryside went up for sale and we had to borrow money to survive. It was dreadful. I attempted to protect my kids from the events that were unfolding, the consequence being that we were losing our home. But the thing that filled me with more sadness and dread than anything else was that my partner and I had decided to split up, once we had sold the property. It was going to be devastating for the kids.

Within the space of less than a year, I had gone from highly sort after, the award-winning film and TV director, amongst the top drama directors in the land, to losing everything I held dear...

➤ My career and vocation

➤ My income and security

➤ My family and friends

➤ My home and sanctuary

➤ My relationship

All wiped out, virtually in the blink of an eye. When I say 'My' I mean 'Our'. My family lost their home and security, too, and there was nothing I could do to prevent it. Believe me, that is a shitload of pain, stress, guilt, worry and regret to take on. Where does one go from there?

Another six months later I was also to 'lose' my kids when they were taken 270 miles away to live in another part of the UK by their mother. I had to do a lot of soul searching and make some profound decisions. One decision, or choice, that I made was that I wasn't going to let what had happened drag me into depression and anxiety. The other decision was a big and scary one - to withdraw from my career in the film and TV world.

One thing I did know at that point was that I never wanted someone else to be in control of whether or not I worked and earned. I would not allow any workplace bully or deceitful TV executive to tarnish my reputation, or question my vast experience and genuine collaborative spirit. I wanted to live and work on my own terms. I also knew that I wanted (and needed) to make an abundance of money, because I'd learned the hard way that lack of money takes away your power of freedom and choice, as well as your family's security and dignity. Having no money sucks. Losing everything sucks.

So I opted out and took the very risky decision to become my own boss and follow my entrepreneurial aspirations. I decided to start an online business, but I had no idea what I was doing or where to begin. This led to a full year of intensive self-education, enhanced by invaluable mentorship and training from some of the best multi-millionaire entrepreneurs in the UK and US digital marketing community. It was a steep learning curve, often scary, but hey, life is one big steep learning curve is it not?

From Drama Queens to Digital Marketing

Spool forward to 2016. If four years ago, someone had told me I'd be a video marketing and advertising specialist and entrepreneur, I wouldn't have believed him. If they'd said that I'd be hanging out with some of the world's most successful digital marketers and talking about traffic, leads, sales, strategy, marketing, video ranking, entrepreneurship, mindset and success principles, I would've laughed at them. If I'd been told that I'd spend more time on YouTube than I do on Netflix and that it would be my business to help business owners, entrepreneurs, marketers, speakers, and coaches to grow their business and channels with online video marketing and advertising strategies, I would've playfully poked them in the eye.

But that is exactly what's occurred. At first, I launched my own local video marketing agency *VideoSeen* and started creating and ranking videos on Google and YouTube for small businesses. I get a huge kick out of helping businesses and marketers get results with video. I'm also a speaker, course creator, and teacher of video marketing. I've been fortunate to have collaborated with some of the best entrepreneurs in the UK and US digital marketing industries, including Paul O'Mahony and Nick James, as well as marketing videos for the likes of Dr. John F. Demartini.

In the last three years, I've learned many lessons about having goals, objectives, and strategies on the road to success. I have learned the power of intention and consistency. I've learned that I never quit, whatever happens. I'm not out of the woods yet; I still have huge financial challenges to overcome and many goals to achieve, not least for the benefit of my teenage kids, who in many respects have 'lost' more than my ex and me.

It's now early 2017 I've been invited to contribute a story, my story, to this book.

It's a huge privilege to be published alongside some of the entrepreneurs I've learned from and collaborate with. I've acquired many valuable lessons over the last three years, which I now apply to my life and business:

> ➤ From crisis comes *opportunity*.

> ➤ Failure is a message to *change*, not a mistake.

> ➤ Nothing is *permanent*.

> ➤ There are *consequences* to every action, decision, and thought.

> ➤ Take full *responsibility* for your thoughts and actions.

> ➤ *Do not blame* anyone else for what happens in your life, good or bad.

> ➤ *Acceptance* is the first step towards letting go of resistance.

I haven't fulfilled my 'supreme' dream to be at the helm a major theatrical motion picture, and that's okay, I guess. There's still time.

As Dr. John F. Demartini said it me recently, *"Everything is as it should be. Do you see that now?"*

 **Andrew Gunn** is an award-winning film and TV director and screenwriter turned online video marketer, YouTube and video advertising specialist. With a background in commercials and high-end TV drama, today Andrew is founder and CEO of video marketing agency and consultancy *VideoSeen* and creator of *Video Traffic Alchemy*. Andrew specializes in Video Marketing, YouTube Marketing, and Online Video Advertising, as a marketer, producer, consultant, and trainer. He helps business owners, entrepreneurs, marketers, speakers, and coaches to produce creative but 'results-driven' campaigns and strategies, so they can grow their businesses and brands with online videos.

During a 25-year career in the British film and television industry, he was fortunate enough to direct some of the most high-profile British shows of recent years, working with Academy Award nominees and BAFTA award-winnersYou might have seen the BAFTA award-winning *LIFE ON MARS*. His hugely successful episode of *DOCTOR WHO ("Victory of the Daleks")* made history with the inception of *Über* Daleks!

FINANCIAL FREEDOM

BRAD SPENCER

"In Character, In Manners, In Style, In All Things, the Supreme Excellence is Simplicity"
- Henry Wadsworth Longfellow

"Financial Freedom" is an elusive state of being that hundreds of books have tried to teach people how to reach. Trying to reach that freedom has frustrated me for years; a lot of the choices I made during my twenties were rooted in the "old" logic of "save, invest, and work your way up." As an entrepreneur, many of those rules either don't apply (since we can create cash flow relatively quickly) or they don't apply in the same way they do for those with traditional jobs.

I have five simple principles that allowed me to reach financial freedom, and I'm going to share them with you. Before we discuss these principles, though, let's get an empowering definition of "Financial Freedom" to work with.

Financial Freedom: The state where your cash flow is greater than your expenses, which allows you to do what you what on your own terms.

Notice that I didn't give you some equation or tell you how to make your money. Financial freedom doesn't require a specific number; it's unique to each of us. The focus on various terminology like "net worth" sabotages you from the result that you really want, which is to live life on your terms.

So, let me ask you this simple question: are you making enough that money doesn't dictate all the choices you make? If so, that's GRRREEEAATTTT (in my best Tony the Tiger voice), but if not, now is your chance to change that.

Bottom line: what you've been told about money and financial freedom has probably held you back from experiencing your ideal life.

Which brings us to our 5 Simple Principles:

1. Be Aware of Feedback Loops in Your Life

A feedback loop is simply a choice which leads to an outcome, which leads to another outcome until you end up at a certain destination.

In a positive feedback loop, your choice leads to a positive outcome, which begets more positive outcomes. Spending less, for example, means you can pay off bad debt, which frees up money to allow you to pay off even more debt until you're debt free.

In a negative feedback loop, your bad choices turn into more bad outcomes. Drug usage is a very simple example; once you start using, you get addicted, your health deteriorates, and so on.

Every choice you make about money creates a "loop" of some sort. It's not always easy to recognize, but a retail therapy habit could be causing a *lot* more problems than you realize, for example.

When you're able to stop the harmful action, eventually the negative loop disappears. Eliminate enough of these harmful habits (like retail therapy, not conforming to a budget, and living off credit) and replace them with positive habits and boom! Your ideal outcome becomes more accessible.

One of the things that wealthy people do is leverage multiple positive loops together. They will, for example, spend less than their means *and* buy investments that increase their cash flow with the difference; their increased earnings from these investments allow them to increase spending, while still acquiring yet more cash-flow producing assets, for example. As a result, the velocity of their wisdom and wealth increases very quickly. This is why the rich get rich and the poor get poorer; one is using positive feedback with their assets.

Action Step: Ask yourself "why am I doing this?" every time you make a financial decision and see what simple solutions you can take to reduce bad habits and increase positive ones.

2. Probabilities Are Your Best Friends Or Worst Enemies

Wealthy entrepreneurs focus on probabilities. How likely is something to happen? If you're worried about something, ask yourself "how likely is the worst case scenario to happen?" It usually isn't as likely as your fear would tell you.

Examining probabilities with new opportunities is essential. Most "opportunities" are traps, distracting you from wealth. You really only need one high probability income stream to create a lifetime of financial freedom. The pursuit of every shiny object is sabotaging you.

Think of the 80/20 rule - 20% of your income streams create 80% of your income. Focus on that 20% exclusively; they're your "high probability" activities. By taking safe, well-planned risks, you'll grow your wealth tremendously. You'll succeed more often, creating more positive momentum than you can shake a stick at.

Action Step: List all the activities you're involved with and how much money they're generating. Ask questions like "How likely will I be to double my income from this?" If it's high, then keep at it. If it's low, drop it.

3. Risk Mitigation...The Less You Lose, The More You Win...

Warren Buffett famously says, "Rule #1... don't lose money...Rule #2.. don't forget Rule #1." This is the mantra of every financially free entrepreneur. The fact is, for every dreamer who takes a giant risk and succeeds, there are 100 dreamers who fall splat on the concrete. Successful entrepreneurs create more wealth and solve problems for their customers while stacking up cash flow day in and day out.

Who do you wanna be?

If you want financial freedom, you need to mitigate your risks for failure as close to zero as possible. Only when you've done that should you take action. I love taking massive action on my dreams, and I might not take as many "swings" as dreamers do, but I win more often. I have way less stress - and more success - because of this.

How do you mitigate risk? Educate yourself, talk to people who've done what you want to do, read biographies of successful people, and hire coaches or consultants. In business, spending a little bit more time and money up front can sometimes save you massive headaches (and an empty checkbook) later on.

Wealthy, financially-free entrepreneurs know and embrace this. There's a direct relationship between someone's financial freedom whether they take "smart risks" instead of "wild dream risks."

Action Step: Examine all the risks in something you're doing. How can you educate yourself or hire someone to solve any potential problem before it exists? How have others before you mitigated these risks? Don't get bogged down overthinking this; the mentality matters more than the specifics.

4. "Everything Is Your Fault" Is the Key to Your Freedom.

Extreme Ownership was a book popular in 2016 with a lot of my friends. It's written by two former Navy SEAL leaders, and I recommend reading it at least once a year.

The main principle in that book is the idea of "Extreme Ownership." My translation of this concept: no excuses, it's all your fault.

Every financial freedom goal a person has will bring up resistance, fear, and excuses. We all deal with this no matter where we are in our journey, and we'll all make mistakes; this is inevitable. You do, however, have a choice. You can blame someone else for something or you can own the mistake or belief and shift to something that is more empowering.

My personal belief is that when you own it all then NO ONE can control you, and this can let you create more freely. Money will follow, because money flows where value is created and rewarded. It's extremely empowering knowing that *everything* I do is caused by a choice or belief I have. If I don't like an outcome, I dig into the actions and beliefs that led to the negative outcome, fix them, and then try again. Adaptability is key.

Action Step: List out everyone or everything you're blaming for anything that you're not happy with. Notice how you feel and ask yourself if there's any other way to look at the situation. Forgive yourself if you made a choice in the past that you wouldn't repeat; we all make mistakes. Own yours so you can move ahead. And purchase the book *Extreme Ownership* - it rocks!

5. 1% A Day Is All You Need To Get Anywhere You Want Financially

This is the most simple principle so far, but it's essential: focus on improving your situation by 1% a day. This might seem trivial, but compounded out, it leads to massive growth, and it's an easy number to focus on.

1% per day growth compounded for a year is 37.78x growth per year. If you started at $100, you'd end up with $3,778 by the end of the year simply by growing 1% a day.

How do you implement this on a practical basis?

I always like to focus on eliminating bad habits, as discussed above. In the past, I used to be bad at saving money. I would always forget to set aside a certain amount each week for a reserve fund. One day, I set up a daily savings account which took $24 from my "spending" fund and put it into my "reserve" fund. At the time, that meant I was saving almost $9,000 a year without noticing it. The amount felt like a stretch for me at first, but I quickly adjusted to it and it became "forgettable."

Another day, I switched a behavior that saved me $1 a day. That was one plane ticket per year for me at the time.

These are simple behavioral shifts that pay off forever.

Being "free" is a state of mind. Financial freedom is the result of a set of daily choices that allow you to do what you want, when you want. Instead of beating yourself up or swinging for the fences, steady improvement of 1% a day on your financial goals will compound and pay dividends quickly.

Action Step: Choose a specific financial goal. Write where you're currently at. Start 1 simple behavior today that will get you to that goal. 1 tiny change is often all it takes to get closer to your financial freedom.

Here's the bottom line: being "financially free" is a choice. Whether you believe it or not, many people choose to stay a slave to their limiting beliefs and status quo because it's hard or scary to change.

This is why so many people peddle crappy "opportunities" that don't work, or, even worse, put you further into debt. It's easy to sell someone who doesn't know what they want.

Many think that money comes in windfalls. It doesn't; wealth is a result of daily choices that compound into an ideal life. I'm always analyzing my choices to see where I'm letting bad choices sabotage my journey in "financial freedom."

 **Brad Spencer** is a former "bricks and sticks" business owner who focuses on creating digital assets that generate consistent sales. He is the "anti-hustle" guy who loves being a dad and helping other people see the greatness in themselves. He's been marketing online since 2008 and has sold millions of dollars of products for himself and clients ranging from entry level product launches, to webinars to high end consulting.

If you want to know more about creating these positive changes and building wealth with simple products and services, visit my site at http://www.8020ProductCreation.com. I have more training and systems you can copy to reach financial freedom with simple products that people want.

"YOU, MY FRIEND, ARE A STARTER, NOT A FINISHER..."

DAVID PERDEW

When he called me out from the stage to answer my simple question with this (*true*) statement, it really ticked me off ... and it was a turning point in my business life!

The Speaker was talking about content creation and productivity.

You know, getting stuff done.

Sitting in the first row, I whined, *"Yes, but my problem is that I have too many ideas and too little time with a dozen projects, and all of them are about 80 percent complete."*

He looked me in the eye, and said, *"You, my friend, are a STARTER, not a FINISHER."*

All of a sudden, I felt the spotlight burning my flesh as this speaker peeled away my excuses to reveal a scared procrastinator.

In front of God, and the other 50 people in that room, he revealed my biggest issue and put a neon flashing light around it for everyone to see.

I was a *wannabe*, not a *doer*. And I knew it.

And I was not happy about it.

But I heard it - loud and clear. And I couldn't get it out of my head.

The Speaker was Craig Perrine. And I'd just met him before he got to the stage.

"Such a nice guy," I thought. And he is, but he wasn't ready to let me off the hook that day. Nope, he was having none of that.

"You, my friend, are a STARTER, not a FINISHER!"

Embarrassed? You bet.

Hurt? Absolutely.

Angry? Oh, you have no idea.

Motivated? Like you wouldn't believe. I would never be called a STARTER again.

The results:

That one statement led me to earn my first $1000 online in just 3 days. But that was 10 years ago.

So, how did being humiliated publicly at a marketing event motivate me to be successful?

First, I'm sure Craig didn't mean to humiliate me. I did a fine job of that myself.

Here's the story.

If you see a bit of yourself here, I hope you'll let me be the one who kicks your butt a little so you, too, can make that big jump to actually getting stuff done...

During one of the longest periods of my life, I had decided that I *might* start a business online.

Notice, I wasn't fully committed, *even though I thought I was.*

I read, studied, listened and totally immersed myself in learning the processes behind making money online.

Learning...

But not doing...

Well, doing just enough to stay in the game, but not really enough to put myself out there and compete.

This was not the first time I bailed on a project because of *"fear of completion."*

The obvious sub-conscious question here is: *What happens when it's done? People will be able to take shots at me and I don't like that.*

I think this is a real problem. And for some of us, it can be hard to overcome because it reinforces our insecurity.

Here's an example:

In 1991, I had my first photography art show. I'd traveled to China and made some beautiful images. I printed about 30 images on 20x24 watercolor paper, framed them in beautiful deep wooden frames and hung them in a gallery for a Saturday night opening.

We sold all the pieces that night - a complete sellout at the opening. The gallery owner was ecstatic. It was a huge success.

The next day, the Sunday paper featured a review of my work and said I couldn't decide whether I wanted to be a photographer or a painter, and neither worked.

I was devastated.

And I knew better. This was a part-time, freelance journalist with zero art training.

Yet, I said I'd never put myself in that position again.

It was my last art show.

And that was crazy because I loved the creative process.

But starting that project (and finishing) had consequences: *People might criticize it.*

It's easy to start. Not so easy to finish. And really easy to quit...

My online business dream was big...make enough money to quit my corporate consulting gig and build an online, multi-million-dollar publishing empire. That seemed out of reach to me, even though I met people every day who were chucking the daily grind for ***The Portable Empire*** as Pat O'Bryan was calling it back then.

Yet, I couldn't make enough to support my habit of buying way too many ebooks, software tools, and memberships. Discouraged, I was fast becoming broke, too.

My wife, ever the brilliant one, said, *"David, when do you know enough? Don't you know enough already to make this work?"*

I was a constant learner. Not much of an implementer.

My thinking shifted because Craig Perrine, the speaker who called me out, had the brass to tell me the truth. And the truth was just enough to jump me into the $1000-per-week success crowd long ago.

He's a really nice guy.

Craig was a featured speaker at Pat O'Bryan's **UnSeminar** in 2005 or 2006 along with Joe Vitale, Bill Hibbler, Jillian Coleman, Nerissa Oden and Ray McNally.

Known as a master listbuilder, I expected Craig to talk about the usual ways of driving traffic to your site: PPC campaigns, joint ventures, affiliate programs, working the forums, and setting up squeeze pages.

But he surprised me by talking about *relationships*.

Those were the Wild West days of Internet Marketing when almost anyone could build a list and use it to extract money. Or at least, that's what they said.

Focusing on relationships to build your business seemed - unnecessary.

But Craig specialized in being personal and real with his subscribers. They knew him and his family because he included real-life experiences in his writing.

So, when he stepped to the stage and began talking about the inner game of marketing (you know, getting your mind right and fighting your own self-limiting demons before you try to convince potential buyers that you've got it all together), I was all ears.

This was exactly what I'd been struggling with for a few years, but especially since the art show a decade before. And it surprised me to hear someone so successful talking so openly about it. From my seat in the front row, I felt like he was talking to me, his newest friend.

I could confide in him … he seemed so sympathetic and gentle.

"I am so confused and scattered," I said. *"I've got so many projects started… How do you complete any when you have so many at 80 percent complete?"*

Listen readers, I hear you.

With a gazillion marketers coming at you with a thousand, panting, "gotta-have-this-now" messages, you may feel like I did.

If you didn't read each email or buy each tool, you'd miss the one that contained the secret.

Surely Craig would share the secret key that would unlock the vault to online riches!

He was my new friend.

We'd made a connection.

Instead, he told me what I didn't want to hear.

It was me. All me. Nobody else. Me.

His answer really ticked me off...

No Guru, no coach, no program, no software - nothing would help me build my online business until two things happened:

1. I had to DECIDE that I wanted to build a business and be committed to it, and...

2. I had to become a STARTER and a FINISHER.

Realize, I had made very few sales because I had nothing in the marketplace.

But Craig's admonition motivated me to make some serious changes.

The result was $1112 in three days.

That was my first $1000 week.

I'd made some money here and there, but nothing consistent, concentrated or predictable.

After spending nearly $22,000 on ebooks, programs, software, and teleseminars, and becoming discouraged and dog-tired, I began to believe that online marketing was a hoax.

The $1000 week changed that too. It was followed by another $1000 week!

That's great, but it wasn't life-changing money. I wanted life-changing money!

When I asked people their level of commitment today, the standard answer is that *"I'm absolutely committed."*

But in reality, most people don't even know what that means.

Being committed means that you're willing to be in the game for the long haul, that you're willing to listen to the people who've been there and done it before you.

And that you're willing, above everything, to be teachable -- NO MATTER WHAT.

If you fail, you learn from it and try again.

If you get discouraged, talk to someone who can help you out of it.

If you don't know the answer to a technical issue, you learn how to use Google to figure it out.

If you're confused about your purpose, you create a roadmap to success that reflects who you are at your core.

No matter what, you never give up. You may adjust. You may adapt. You may even get a job to improve your finances. If you want more consistency with your finances, you might keep your job.

But you'll never give up, and you're willing to do what's necessary. That's commitment.

One of my favorite movies from the 1980s is ***Body Heat*** with William Hurt (as Racine), Kathleen Turner (as Matty Walker), and Richard Crenna (as Edmund Walker).

Racine is obsessed with Matty, but Matty is married to Edmund Walker. Luckily, Edmund travels a lot, and Racine and Matty spend a lot of time together.

There is one scene I'll never forget. Racine walks into the local restaurant because he sees Matty. He plops down beside her and the man she's with only to discover that the man is her husband, Walker.

This is the conversation (From Lawrence Kasdan's 1980 screenplay, ***Body Heat***):

WALKER: *You wouldn't believe the dorkus she was with when I met her. The guy came to us with a business proposition. We're always looking for opportunities. If the conditions are right. We're willing to take an occasional risk if the downside isn't too steep. But this guy hadn't done his homework, he didn't know the bottom line. That's how I knew he was full of it. You've got to know the bottom line. That's all that really counts...*

WALKER: *He didn't have the goods, this guy. He was like a lot of guys you run into -- they want to get rich, they want to do it quick, they want to be there with one score.*
But they're not willing to do what's necessary. Do you know what I mean?

RACINE (Racine looks at him in silence for a moment.): *I'm not sure. You mean, lay the groundwork? Earn it?*

WALKER: *No. I mean do what's necessary.*
Whatever's necessary.

After that conversation, Racine was willing to do whatever was necessary. Watch the movie to find out what that was… I won't spoil it for you.

Until I was called a STARTER, I was not willing to do what was necessary!

So when people come to me frustrated, moaning about their situation, I do have empathy for them because I've been there and I understand how terrible it feels.

But someone went beyond the empathy with me and told me the hard truth.

Who's going to tell you the truth?

If you're not willing to put in the work, to do whatever is necessary to be successful, then it's not going to happen.

And that's the truth.

Doing business, online or offline, is not easy. Most people will tell you that it is.

I won't.

The easy thing is to always give up.

Those who don't are the winners.

They are the ones who go to the bank every week and increase their account with this week's earnings of $10, $100, $1000, and more.

And they finish what they start.

Which are you? Starter, or Finisher?

 **David Perdew**, CEO and founder of NAMS - the Novice to Advanced Marketing System. He's a journalist, consultant and serial entrepreneur who has built one of the most successful and fastest growing business training systems online today called the MyNAMS Insiders Club.

The Novice to Advanced Marketing System is a step-by-step system focusing on Team, Training and Tools to help novice to advanced business people build a Simple, Scalable and Sustainable business.

He took a year off in 2003 to personally build a 2200 square foot log cabin in north Alabama where he and his wife and two dogs and a cat live on 95 acres of forest with four streams and a 60-foot waterfall. http://nams.ws/trial

How Two "Wrongs" Made A Really Big "Right"

Steve Sipress

Today, I help clients in all different types of small businesses, all over the world, put effective sales and marketing strategies and systems into use, with outstanding results. I've become one of the most-respected, most highly-paid, most sought-after small business marketing consultants in the world.

But none of that would have been possible without two major negative events occurring in my life.

1. The Only Test I Ever Flunked

I was an excellent student all through high school and then college, graduating with honors from a top liberal arts university. A friend took the Law School Admission Test, and got a great score. So I figured I would do well on it, too.

I was right. I scored in the 99th percentile, and got into a top law school. I never really wanted to be a lawyer, but I definitely wanted to stay in school and avoid the real world for another three years, so off I went.

I treated my three years in law school pretty much the same as I had my previous four years in college: working various part-time jobs, skipping classes, hanging out with friends, and not cracking a textbook until the very end of every semester. That nonsense had worked okay to get me through my undergraduate days, but when it came to law school, I just barely passed with enough credits to earn my law degree.

After graduation, all of my classmates spent their summer taking full-time prep classes and studying for the bar exam. Meanwhile, I chose to work a full-time job and study on my own once in awhile – saving money by using the previous year's review guides. But I was hardly "reviewing" anything, since I hadn't taken many of the courses to begin with, and had barely studied the subjects I did take. "How could I not pass the bar exam?" I thought. "I'm smart, I went to a top school, and I've always aced exams my whole life, even when I didn't study hard."

Oops.

A few months later, the results of the bar exam arrived in the mail. Sure enough, I had flunked it. (I missed by only a single point – but it's a pass/fail test, so I failed.)

Sure, my heart wasn't ever really in working as a lawyer, but now that door was slammed shut, right in my face. My entire "do-as-little-as-necessary-to-get-by" attitude that I was so proud of for the first 25 years of my life had proven to be a faulty approach to success.

I was shocked and devastated for a few days, wondering what I was going to do next. One thing I knew for sure: *I promised myself I would never do anything half-assed ever again. I would do everything 100% all out, or I wouldn't do it at all.*

2.   A Multi-Million Dollar Business Down The Drain

So there I was. I was now 25 years old, done with a lifetime of schooling, and wondering what the heck to do with my life.

Just then, a friend showed me some obscure classified ads he had found where people were charging money to run fantasy sports leagues – something I had started doing as a hobby during my final year of law school, as a way to keep in touch with friends and family. We all thought I had invented the game, because back then none of us had heard of anyone running such games professionally.

"Could I really make a living doing something I love?" I thought. "How great would it be to be able to turn my hobby into a business?" I decided to go for it.

Remembering my vow to myself to put in 100% effort, I put everything I had into starting and building my new business. I even went back for a few weeks to working the job I had in high school – hustling around the seats at Madison Square Garden selling beer and popcorn – to earn enough money to buy a computer, print up some brochures, and place a classified ad of my own.

The ad worked, my game was a hit, and I was off and running as an entrepreneur!

Thanks to a ton of hard work plus some extremely effective marketing strategies, within just three years my company was the largest in the fledgling industry. My revenues were basically doubling in size every year, as were the size of my office, the amount of my equipment, and the number of my employees. Life was hectic but good!

Then one day, one of my customers approached me with a business proposition. He brokered a deal with a major investor where I would get an influx of capital, as the first step towards taking the company public. Back then, I knew absolutely nothing about how business really works, so I made a HUGE mistake. I turned it down.

The proposal was $1.75 million in exchange for 45% of my company. The terms would have allowed me to stay in control of my business, and the cash would have allowed me to hire more staff, acquire more equipment, ramp up my marketing, AND finally take a little bit for myself to end my years of continually pouring every dime and every minute I had back into my company. Most important of all, I would have had expert guidance from successful, experienced business people who knew how to properly run and grow a business.

So what went through my mind? Here's my completely wrong thinking:

I figured that if someone would pay me $1.75 million for less than half of my company, then it was already worth more than $3.5 million. And if I had built it from scratch to worth $3.5 million in just a little over three years, then wouldn't it be worth about $10 million after 10 years? And then wouldn't I rather have 100% of a $10 million company instead of just 55% of it?

Back then, that actually seemed to make sense to me. How naïve I was!

My business continued to double every year, but I was reinvesting everything back into my business to fuel the furious growth, and was still working long hours, taking no vacations, and trying to figure out everything all by myself. I was running leagues in six different sports, and they all overlapped, leaving no downtime in between one season and the next.

Then it happened. I hit the dreaded wall that all entrepreneurs hit at some point: The excitement of the "building" and "establishing" phase started to give way to more mundane – albeit necessary – responsibilities. The business continued to grow, but I found myself spending less and less time and energy on it. That sounds like a good thing, and it's certainly a valid goal for all entrepreneurs. In fact, it's exactly what I help my clients do today, by putting effective marketing systems into place.

However, back then, I didn't have any real systems in place – I was relying on good old fashioned hard work, and constantly running on all cylinders with the pedal to the metal. I was constantly innovating and increasing my marketing and advertising in order to stay ahead of the competition.

But I made a huge, fatal mistake: I did it all on my own, basically by the seat of my pants. I didn't have a mentor or board of directors to help guide me. As a result, I made a lot of mistakes, worked much harder than I should have had to, and left a ton of money on the table. I was under constant stress, and started to get burned out.

Then, after six years of fast and steady growth, a major roadblock came up: The Major League Baseball spring training lockout of 1990, which threatened to cancel the entire season. My entire source of revenue for six months would be gone, although, of course, most of my expenses would continue to have to be paid.

The labor issue was settled only one week into the season, but the damage was done. I suffered about a six-figure loss in advertising and marketing costs, and for the first time ever, my revenues were lower than in the past, thanks to not having enough time to take on new customers and set up new leagues in between the end of the lockout and the start of the season.

Navigating this setback without any experienced guidance proved to be too big of a challenge for me to overcome all on my own. The entire multi-million dollar business went into a tailspin, and collapsed just a few months later, taking everything I owned with it.

I promised that from then on, I would dedicate myself to learning how business really works, and I would set up future businesses based on systems, and with plenty of expert guidance.

I set off learning all about business, with a focus on the area where all of the revenue comes from: effective marketing. The more books I read, conferences I attended, courses I took, and guidance I got, the more I realized that I had already used many innovative and effective marketing strategies to grow my multi-million dollar business.

I also learned one other key fact: Everyone teaching how to market a small business had a tendency to make everything overly complex and mysterious. I later met many of these "marketing gurus," and learned that this was actually all by design: By making effective small business marketing seem complicated and difficult, they gave themselves job security. Business owners would always need to buy more and more of their materials, attend more and more of their conferences, and pay them for more and more of their personal advice.

That's why I invented **The WOW! Strategy™.**

I took everything I had learned from all of the "gurus," after investing nearly $300,000 of my own money and putting in years of studying and trial-and-error, and boiled it down to one simple strategy that every small business owner can easily implement. They get only three things right, and their days of frustration, stress, and up-and-down revenue and profits are over forever.

Over the years, I've helped thousands of small business owners implement **The WOW! Strategy™** in their businesses, with amazing, life-changing results.

I have assembled a team of marketing experts to help my clients put effective marketing systems and strategies into place, and to act as their board of directors to guide them through the inevitable ups and downs of being a small business owner or entrepreneur. As a result of having such effective systems and team members, I can give all of my clients a 100% Money-Back Guarantee they will get results.

My clients (and especially their spouses!) thank me for transforming their lives, by taking away their stress and frustration, while at the same time increasing their revenues and profits. That is tremendously satisfying to me.

It's something I never could have done, and a life I never could have built, if I hadn't learned two very powerful lessons from the two most "negative" experiences of my life.

I hope all small business owners gain the wisdom that I did from going through these painful times, without having to experience that type of pain themselves.

Steve Sipress is the founder and President of Successful Selling Systems, Inc., and is widely recognized as one of the world's highest-paid and most respected small business marketing consultants. He is known for getting transformational results for his clients, and is the only marketing consultant who backs up his guidance, strategies, and systems with a 100% Money-Back Guarantee.

Over the past 30+ years, he has created and built over a dozen successful companies, and has consistently helped his clients improve their incomes and lifestyles by teaching and implementing innovative, out-of-the-box sales, marketing, and general business strategies that work far beyond anyone's expectations, in every conceivable industry and situation, and no matter what the state of the economy, or the time of year, or the physical location of the business.

He is the creator of the simple and powerful *The WOW! Strategy™ - How To Solve ALL Of Your Small Business Sales And Marketing Problems,* which he has used to help thousands of small business owners, has taught in high-level workshops, and is about to be published as his 24th book.

Steve has written numerous articles on sales and marketing for a wide range of publications, has appeared on radio and television, is an accomplished and entertaining speaker, and has a following of tens of thousands of raving fans online and off.

He is the publisher of *The Rhino Daily Podcast, The Rhino Daily Blog,* and *Rhino Monthly Magazine,* as well as the co-creator and co-star of the *Lessons Learned From Donald Trump Podcast* – all of which provide valuable advice for small business owners and entrepreneurs.

He has earned the nickname "Straight-Talk Steve" for his no-nonsense, results-oriented, problem-solving approach to business and success. As a bonus for reading this chapter, get a free one-hour one-on-one strategy session ($1200 value) where Steve will help you implement *The WOW! Strategy™* into your business by going to: www.SteveSipress.com/heroes

SIGHTING IN THE RIFLE

BRANDON RICHEY

"Mistakes are always forgivable, if one has the courage to admit them."
—Bruce Lee

I remember as a kid growing up I started out playing baseball. My dad would take me to the park and hit fly balls to me for what seemed like hours as I would run from one side of the field to the other to chase them down. This was a far cry from today where many kids would rather spend those hours on the Xbox at home sitting on the couch.

One thing my parents always instilled in both me and my brother was hard work…and smart work! You see both me and my brother grew up working at my dad's service station, which he still has today in Toccoa, Georgia. We would spend long hot summer days working on cars, doing oil changes, brake jobs, changing tires, pumping gas, washing trucks, and doing just about anything else that needed to get done.

The hours were long and the summer days were unforgiving with the sweltering Georgia heat. Since both of us played football and baseball we would work between sport seasons as much as possible and would even continue on sometimes during college.

Working such long hours as a young teenager taught me a lot about the value of money and responsibility. It was something I didn't necessarily always enjoy at the time, but ultimately it would be a huge life lesson.

Even though I had a fairly solid athletic career, my sports playing days were cut short at the beginning of my senior season in football due to having suffered an ACL, meniscus cartilage, and medial collateral ligament tear of my right knee in the season opener. It was a devastating injury.

Regardless, after my athletic career was abruptly ended with a traumatic knee injury I would still find time to hone my fitness and hit the weight room five days a week. I literally had a schedule of work, train, eat, shower, bed, and repeat.

I was now staring down a college career and not yet 100% sure of the direction I wanted to take my life. Sure, I had planned on going into the field of education as a teacher and a coach, but looking back, I wasn't quite sure of this path when I started.

The First Stage Of Sighting In My Rifle

It was during this stage of my life I first started to feel like I was having a bit of a difficult time sighting in my rifle (metaphorically speaking). To clarify what I mean by this if you've ever sighted in a rifle you already know bullets don't travel in a straight line, but, rather, in an arc.

The bullet's path is affected by gravity, therefore the sights must be adjusted so the path of the bullet can be accurate to the target at a given distance. To pull this off, you basically take aim at a target, fire your round, and evaluate where on the target you were able to hit, if you were able to hit the target at all.

Well, up to this point, I started recognizing that I had dropped a few rounds out of the chamber and I still wasn't near the bullseye. I felt uncertain of the path I had chosen, but talked myself into moving along it despite my internal doubt.

Once again I found myself in a position of doing some soul searching as to what I wanted to do with my life. After I charged through physical therapy and got my knee better, I eventually went on to attend college at UGA talking myself into going down the path of teaching and coaching even though it was something I wasn't completely sold on doing.

I had enrolled into the School of Education. Despite this, during college I had fortunately kept pursuing my love of fitness through developing my own level of strength. I also found myself regularly falling back to read different books on bodybuilding and strength training to satisfy my growing curiosity. This part of my life remained consistent even though at the time I felt my career might be heading in a different direction.

Even though I had completed my 3rd year of college in the School of Education at UGA, I found myself to be unhappy. I really just wanted to coach and wasn't that enthused about having to sit in a classroom all day long just to coach a few hours at the end of the day after school.

Now, don't get me wrong - there's nothing wrong this, and we need good coaches and teachers, but this dance in particular just wasn't for me. I finally started getting honest with myself and internally I knew I had been lying to myself all along regarding what I really wanted to do with my life.

Firing Another Round At My Education Target

I also wasn't happy in the School of Education at UGA because I found myself having a strong disagreement with what they were teaching in their curriculum. It wasn't as much about truth and history as it was about victimization and a sort of indoctrination. I could spend the time to get a lot more political here, but that's a discussion for another day.

So even though I was facing the loss of two years worth of credit for changing my major, I did it anyway. At the same time, even though I was making a change, I felt that I had somehow failed by throwing away three key years of my life with school.

I don't like to burn bridges, but due to the combination of several major letdowns from the school, I literally made a strong statement to the School of Education department head by essentially telling them *to shove it.* I did this after a heated disagreement that had been building for weeks over certain matters concerning the dishonesty and inconsistency of my teacher in grading a couple of my exams. Looking back, I had gone through another round trying to sight in my rifle here as well, concerning my education goals.

At this point, I set my target and walked across the street to the School Of Health And Human Performance. Long story short - I was happy enough with the decision and never looked back.

Firing Rounds To Sight In My Rifle For My Career Path

Fast forward to graduating from college, and I started training at a Gold's Gym in Lilburn, Ga. It was strictly a commission-based pay job and what a wake-up call that was to me!

It usually shocks people when I tell them that I've literally never had a salary job my entire career since graduating college. In addition to this, what I found in the fitness industry was that nobody wanted to commit to anything on the client side, and the money in this business starting out was certainly very hard to come by.

Once again, I felt I'd hit a roadblock in my life. My journey started looking to have a certain trend with these roadblocks, or obstacles, and I was realizing I was still having a difficult time sighting in my rifle to hit the target.

During this time, I was able to connect back to my roots at UGA by contacting a good friend of mine, Bryan Pulliam (recent Georgia State Director of NSCA) who was at the time an assistant to the strength and conditioning program at UGA for the football team. At the time, Dave Van Halanger was the head strength coach and Bryan had put a good word in for me to volunteer, to come down and meet with him.

Coach Van Halanger was very kind and allowed me to come to team workouts to gain more experience of the program and to work with the athletes at the D-1 level. This was exciting.

At the same time this was going on, I was also looking at another coaching facility that existed in Gwinnett County. They specialized in athletic performance development for athletes of every kind. The program was headed up by Gary Schofield, (the current Southeast Regional Coordinator for NSCA) and we would train athletes for performance, regardless of their sport.

As I was setting my sights on this particular venture, tragedy struck again with a second traumatic knee injury to my other knee. I was in the middle of a training drill performing bounds which I had done numerous times before, and suffered a 100% rupture in my patella tendon. I'll never forget that one as it sounded like a shotgun going off inside my head when it popped and my kneecap literally shot up into my thigh like a tensioned rubber band snapping in half.

Once again, I was faced with the disappointment of injury interfering with a career path that I had been working on growing. I was sighting in my rifle, but as it turns out, the process of recovering from this injury taught me a lot about myself and a great deal about performance training. Looking back, it was this particular round that was actually getting me closer to hitting my bullseye.

It was in the recovery process, during and after this injury, that I gained vast experience in plyometric training, speed, and agility training. This sort of completed the model for what I could combine with my current strength program. I would eventually move on from this job to start my own business.

In 2005 I had failed at running two different training facilities. I had jumped in early on in the business and got caught up in a subleasing situation, with my lease being with business owners that were very unethical and people that I would rather have never met.

That was a very difficult situation financially, emotionally, and mentally for me. I knew I couldn't go through such a loss like that again, and realized I had to restructure my business model to allow me to operate with assurances so that others (like those crooks I had the lease with) couldn't impact me, or my business operation negatively.

So, I started contracting with small groups, organizations, and individual clients. Additionally, I started looking for other impactful ways to market my services and broaden my reach to others in the most positive way. I was fortunate enough to have met a good friend of mine and the lead author of this book, Matt Bacak, who eased me into writing and marketing.

I simply started training him as I did with many of my other clients and after some time, he suggested I try some different things to market my services. In 2009 the Brandon Richey Fitness site was published. I know what you're thinking - Matt asked me to say that...No, he didn't. I have always been straightforward and honest about how I started the online portion of my business and Matt had a big part in it.

In Closing

I've been fortunate and have had a very interesting career. Over the years I've spent time training with world class athletes. I was able to work with my good friend Jeff Perry back in 2003 by helping him with his strength program to defend his national title in Muay Thai kickboxing. He succeeded, and ever since I've also been his student for Muay Thai while also developing the strength programs for many fighters.

I also became a contributing author to the huge online fitness magazine Breaking Muscle and the Brandon Richey Fitness blog was listed as one of the Top 10 Best Fitness Blogs on the internet in 2015 by Breaking Muscle. Hopefully. I can make another run at it here in 2017.

In the past year I've also become the leading Sports Ambassador for a brand new topical pain reliever called Cobrazol Sport which I'm working to break into regional and national distribution. It's a beast of a venture, but it's already starting to happen on a local scale.

The truth is that I try to show others how to sight in their rifles the way I have, but I'm also always working to sight my rifle in for other areas of my life. The truth is over the years I've fired many rounds and have faced much disappointment with missed targets concerning business, relationships, and money.

Despite all the good things, I am always reminding myself and others that working to hit the bullseye takes work in every aspect of our lives. I'm currently working on that very thing concerning some personal aspects of my own life. Truthfully, it's a never-ending task, but it's a skill that can be acquired by everyone...as long as we have the will to keep loading in the ammunition. Stay strong!

Brandon Richey, B.S.,CSCS.

Strength & Conditioning Coach, Author

Founder Of Brandon Richey Fitness LLC

Head Sports Ambassador For Cobrazol Sport

FORTUNE FAVORS THE BOLD

BARB LING

Blood.

Lots of blood, actually.

True that said blood WAS contained within a blood-collecting device…

… and that particular blood-collecting device was being deftly held by a smiling surgeon who could have graced the cover of *Gentleman's Quarterly*…

But I'm getting ahead of myself.

Let me ask you now to lean back, close your eyes, then open them again so you can actually read the enchanting story of "If it's going to happen to ANYONE, it will happen to Barb Ling" and let's begin!

I've been an extremely successful online marketer now for 20+ years. Started back in 1997 when I was hailed as the only 5-star resource by Inc. Magazine regarding Internet Recruiting Training, broke the Google code in 2004 and was able to rank in the top 3 for any keyword imaginable, on pages monetized with eBay, Amazon, Adsense and Clickbank [my 2nd 250K year!], and then…..

Well, then I basically went underground and focused on raising my four kids, two moose (okay rescue dogs), bunches of budgies and the like.

Life was delightful….Until that time in August 2011 when said life ferociously kicked me in the teeth.

And, wow, did that ever hurt!* * *

I had failed at something….

Bigtime. Massively. Dramatically. Hollywood Blockbuster Epic Worthy.

See, I miscalculated some rather important things that caused past actions of mine to self-combust into a blindingly brilliant flaming ball of doom.

With neon highlights to boot.

Obviously, I'm nothing, if not an overachiever. But I digress. Anywhos!

I had two choices! I could either:

> ➤ Feel miserable! or

> ➤ Take that energy and propel in bunches of monetary goodness!

Due to the fact I was hormonal, I of course opted for the first reaction and indulged myself in a bout of self-pity that would make emo 3-year-olds weep with admiration!

Seriously, though, while I still had bunches of healing regarding ghosts of my past, I did give myself plenty of time to honor my feelings and emotions….**that gave me the strength to finally let them go.**

Once that was over, I decided to be….a wee bit…productive.

And to move forward in the best way that would power *me*. Here's what I did.

1.) First….I decided to share what I had learned. I wrote:

> ➤ Knowing WHEN to Fold – Key Life Skill

> ➤ Tell Yourself Today – Pass It On

> ➤ Tell yourself today – Shun Stupidity

> ➤ Tell Yourself Today – True Gift Horses Can…

> ➤ Tell Your Child Today – Tone It Down

Why I did this: If there's one thing my decades of living has taught me, it's passing on what I learn is one of the greatest actions I can do during me life.

I truly believe that what goes around, comes around…and proactively being there either for my readers, my friends, my family….it's a Good Thing indeed.

2.) Next, I took my wasted effort…and put it to good use.

Awhile back, I had built The Hero Within You – a site that was meant to provide positive cheer to someone. Alas, it backfired quite dramatically. These things happen.

So…..I revamped the site and dedicated it towards my inner hero, that aspect of my personality which compels me to do the right thing and look out for others ahead of my own self-interests.

I updated the header image to include my guardian animal spirit, added social networking buttons, and (love this part) monetized each page.

Why I did this: I chose to do this action because it validated my intentions of a Good Thing. The fact it now benefits me, instead of someone else…that's just an added bonus (because quite frankly, I tend to put myself last in many situations. I'm working on this, never fear).

Plus…it's making a direct statement to my inner spirit – I had done what I viewed was a Good Thing. It still is a Good Thing…and it's something I simply choose not to regret. Woot!

3.) Then, I decided to transform the excess energy into cold hard cash.

I perused the latest of quality info products out there, and settled on:

15 Pre-Monetized "Done for you" Niche Sites

It was a great product for people who didn't want to write their own info-product.

After the first day of promoting it, I cleared 3 figures.

This made me very happy indeed.

Why I did this: When you feel like hell, you have two choices.

You can either wallow in self-pity (which is actually quite enjoyable sometimes)…or **you can tell the world, "f*ck that bleep, I'm going to succeed."**

After my well-deserved pity party, I dove kneecap-first into the second option.

My Paypal balance is quite thrilled indeed.

4.) After that, I revisited Warrior Forum.

I used to be quite active there!

I took several hours to wander about and reacquaint myself and realized, hmmmm, here is a forum in which I can definitely both share my knowledge and also build my marketing network.

So I checked out my previous signature and saw it simply went back to my site. Not good enough, decreed I….so, like my Twelcome to Twitter page, I built my Welcome Fellow Warrior! page.

Why I did this: The Warrior Network consists of both seasoned and newbie marketers. Thus, it only makes sense that **I should offer a personal greeting** that is tailored to their needs. Check it out…you'll see what I mean.

5.) Finally, I revamped my email marketing/newsletters.

To be honest, I really have dropped the ball with staying in contact with my lists. I made a commitment to myself to fix that.

Back then, I had two main lists; on Monday, I sent out my sale of the week, and on Thursday, I reminded people of that, plus gave them humor, insights and the like.

I did the same thing for the other list, only on Tuesdays and Fridays.

This has resulted in my Paypal balance steadily increasing (love it when that happens!).

Why I did this: Money.

I like it. You do too, I'll bet!

And this is how I returned to Internet Marketing… back in Sept of 2011.

Your takeaways? Life will ALWAYS happen… You've got 2 ways to deal with it. Get smooshed by it…

Or take that horribly crushing negative energy and direct it into something that will make you money soon.

So why did I start this chapter about blood? It happened the next year, in 2012.

In August of 2012, I was invited by Dennis Becker to speak at his Las Vegas event.

And I did! It was amazingly grand too… met lots of brilliant entrepreneurs and gained tremendous insights into how marketing was evolving at that time.

On the very last day (the day I was scheduled to return home), I remember sitting at my sleek 1980-modern hotel room desk (it was about 4am?) and …

(I hope you're sitting down for this)

Stretching my left foot.

A nice common action, wouldn't you say?

Thing is, there was a millisecond of "hmmm, something feels weird" that happened right before… **My foot fell off.**

Okay, it didn't really fall off, but apparently, my foot bones managed to grind themselves onto one another during the stretch (called "bone on bone agony")…

…. Which resulted in my inability to put any substantial weight on it.

Now, imagine the following.

You're at a glorious Internet marketing event, the host is scheduled to fly home on the same flight as you, you manage to hobble your way to the hotel lobby, and greet said host with "You'll never believe this but I can barely walk longer than 2.8 seconds without excruciating pain!"

I will admit – I certainly did get to know Dennis Becker quite well! BTW, he is a gem of a person – smart, down to earth, and very caring to boot.

Somehow I did manage to get back to NJ…

… and ended up having my ankle fused two months later (7 individual surgeries and I now carry more hardware in my ankle than Home Depot. You can see the somewhat graphic pix at http://askbling.com/fusedankle (not to mention the extremely gorgeous surgeon holding the blood collecting device).

And what's happened since then?

Well, I have more nonoptimal times than optimal…

… and I have to squoosh in my marketing activities during those times I'm "good" compared to "godawful".

Eh, life happens. I'm still above ground!

Your takeaway? If your physical health doesn't make "normal" possible…

Turn on a dime and craft your business into something you can do during the times you are capable of work.

And what if you want to start succeeding in Internet Marketing…today?

You need to pick your niche, start small… and work your way up.

Let's take, oh, I don't know… product creation.

The first thing you need to do is network with your future colleagues…. (and here I will bet you thought I'd say make a product!).

Join many of the popular JVzoo/W+ product launch groups and some of the general "how to I start marketing" groups. Introduce yourself. If marketing questions are asked, go to Google to search out the answers and then share them to get your name known.

Every day, take note of who wins the W+ Deal of the Day award and the JVzoo Product of the Day award… and publicly congratulate them/tag them on your FB line.

Make it so you're not just an unknown name… but someone who is worth knowing.

See, the vast majority of product creators make their sales NOT by their efforts… but by the efforts of affiliates who promote them.

So get known by them.

Then, get your feet wet by creating quick low-cost offer at W+.

I myself create one-page cheat sheets that I generally sell between $3 and $4. You can learn how to create offers over at:

·   http://askbling.com/wplusoffer

Get yourself used to how the system works.

(If you need an upsell, which I highly recommend, invest in one of the done-for-you PLR and PLR Businesses in Boxes you can find over at JVzoo:

·   http://askbling.com/plrjvz

Customize that by adding your name and claiming it as your own… and then add those as your upsells (lots of the businesses-in-boxes come with video training as well that show you how to upload them to your site)).

And while you're doing all of the above…

… let your colleagues on FB know you are embarking on this adventure. When you are starting out, it doesn't matter how many copies you sell…

It matters that you build up your self-confidence by taking action and making things happen.

Thank the people who have helped you…. and then rinse and repeat.

Again and again and again and again.

Because that's how you kick fate in the right direction – you take action and make things happen.

In closing: Just about anyone can become successful in Internet marketing. It all depends on how much permission you give yourself to succeed… no matter how much learning is required.

Remember… Fortune Favors the Bold.

Go out and make yourself fortunate… today!

Barb Ling is an unrepentant maverick Internet marketing veteran who enjoys coffee, gymizing even though handicapable, moose-rassling and providing encouragement and motivation to anyone who simply wants to take control of their own destiny.

A spouse of 25 years, Mom to a plethora of kids and Chief Moose Wrangler (aka rescue dogs), she specializes in always being the first to cash in on future trends (for example, she cleared over 22K from a $3.77 cheatsheet product about Pokemon Go).

She offers a Daily Morning Perkup over at her flagship site:

http://barbaraling.com

That covers the daily state of the marketing world (not to mention her never-ending adventures in Lingland) and also gives you free admission to her 4-week long Marketing Lingsights class (Get it? Insights? LINGsights? HAHAHAHAHAHAHA coffee. Must have more coffee).

You can follow her on FB at http://askbling.com/btlfb and remember: Everyone has failed mind-reading 101. Introduce yourself and say hi and what you think about her Lingsights… today!

BELIEVE IN YOURSELF

SHARI FRIEDMAN

Something happens in most of us when we reach the age of 40 that seems to be a turning point.

We're older, wiser and have more clarity about what we want and don't want with regard to where we are in life.

We tend to look at our health and fitness, our relationships, our finances, and whether or not we're happy with where we are.

Like most of us, 40 was a turning point in my life. I was overweight, unhappy with my marriage and in a 9-5 job I hated.

Fortunately, I had turned to fitness as my vice and a way to release the stress and unhappiness I was feeling.

Through the help of a personal trainer, I had begun losing weight and slowly watched my body taking a shape I never thought I could possibly achieve.

A Life Changing Transformation

As my body transformed, I had decided to enter a physique competition.

To take on such an endeavor takes focus, drive, determination and consistency. You need absolute commitment to your workouts and diet. There is no missing a workout and the diet is very strict. There is no cheating on your diet, no failing to have your meals prepared, and strict adherence to eating on a schedule.

Although I did not place at the competition, having gone through the journey to be standing up on that stage was a moment of pride for me.

Going through this process, was more than a physical transformation. It was a life changing transformation.

It had caused me to dig deep within myself and discover what I was made of. It taught me that I could achieve anything I put my mind to. More importantly, it taught me to believe in myself.

In the process, I had also discovered a new passion and purpose in my life. Fitness. And it was a way for me to start making some changes in my life.

In less than a year after the show, I had gotten certified as a Personal Trainer, had taken a leap of faith and quit my day job. I had now joined the ranks of the self-employed.

For the first time, I felt like my life had purpose and meaning.

Over the next few months, I had begun building my brand and my clientele. However, I knew that it was time for me to once again believe in myself and take another life changing leap of faith - I ended my marriage of close to 20 years.

This was the first time I was truly on my own and I was scared.

I had discovered internet marketing and saw how there were a few people in the fitness industry making money selling digital products online who had also begun building up a social media following when Facebook took over MySpace as the social media platform of choice.

I was intrigued at what these "fitness info-preneurs" were doing and began building up my brand on Social Media. Through Facebook, I had connected with some of the top Clickbank info-preneurs in the fitness industry.

Once again, I believed in myself, took a leap of faith, and created my first online product, Transformation Over 40.

If these people were doing it, there was no reason why I couldn't. They all started at the same place I was currently.

I knew nothing about how to go about doing this. I knew nothing about marketing or copywriting. All I knew was that I couldn't worry about the how. I had to trust that it would all come together.

A Life Changing Email

One day, I received an email from one of the fitness info-preneurs I follow; actually, I was one of his affiliates. Turns out he has an online digital marketing and publishing company that was growing and was looking to hire someone.

I immediately replied to his email. If I had to create the perfect opportunity, this was it. This email changed the direction of my career in the industry and taught me the inner workings of just about every aspect of digital marketing.

I found a new passion and purpose. I fell head over heels in love with online marketing and being part of a dynamic team.

This company was doing well, growing, and I become a key player on the team.

I believed in this company so much, that after a year, I knew it was time for me to take another leap of faith. I left the gym, and dedicated myself to working full time with this company.

After wearing several different hats, I had found my role. I became part of the email marketing team writing email copy for some of the biggest names in the online fitness industry.

If you would have told me five years ago that I'd be an email copywriter and that I would love doing that, I would've thought you were crazy.

After three years, sadly, that company I was with disbanded. For the first time in over 20 years, I found myself with no income, writing a resume as an email copywriter and began reaching out to some of the biggest names in the fitness industry as well as the self-help / self-improvement space.

Today, I work behind the scenes, writing emails and article content for some the best of the best in the fitness and self-improvement industry.

Another first!

Over the years, I have followed some of the biggest names in the Internet Marketing space and through social media, have been networked with them for the past few years.

Much to my surprise, for the first time, I had been invited to do a training about email copywriting for one of the biggest and most respected names in the Internet Marketing space.

I had never done a training like this before, and to be asked by this particular person was an honor.

I felt as though I had just stepped into another dimension - being officially recognized as an expert as an email copywriter.

This experience has encouraged me to take the next leap of faith and come out of the shadows to begin creating my own products in the email marketing niche.

Life's Biggest Lesson

I can honestly say that none of these events would have transpired had I not put myself through the grueling journey of transforming my body and stepping on that stage which had taught me one of life's biggest lessons… *To Believe In Yourself.*

Shari (Fitness) Friedman is considered by many, one of the top fat-loss over 40 experts in the fitness industry, helping thousands of men and women over 40 lose weight and get their health and fitness back.

Like so many others, 40 became a turning point in her life where she not only transformed her body but transformed her life.

Shari is not only known as a fat-loss over 40 expert, she has also become one of the top email copywriters for some of the biggest names in the fitness and self-help space such as Elliott Hulse, Vince Del Monte, Coach Scott Abel, Steve G. Jones, The Lean Kitchen Queen as well as writing content for Critical Bench. She also does consulting for those who are new to online marketing.

TransformationOver40.com

THE ULTIMATE SACRIFICE

RON WHITE

He pointed to the wall behind me and said, 'I don't know how you did that.'

I pointed to the Congressional Medal of Honor around his neck and replied, 'It was a lot easier than doing that.'

A year or so later, in a wooded area outside of Dallas, surrounded by military veterans, a younger equivalent-version of this warrior, whose eyes were searching the same wall, hit me on the shoulder and proclaimed, 'That's some good shit.'

He was reading the names of his friends.

Medal of Honor recipient Lt Michael Murphy

Petty Officer Second Class Danny Dietz

Petty Officer Matthew Axelson

They were three of the four SEALs who lost their lives on Operation Red Wing in the Hindu Kush mountains of Afghanistan in the summer of 2005. These members of a four man SEAL team had been inserted to find a Taliban leader, Ahmad Shah who was responsible for the death of at least 20 Marines.

Murphy, Dietz and Axelson were ambushed by dozens of Taliban when their position was compromised by sheep herders who had stumbled upon their position.

Lt. Michael Murphy was posthumously awarded the military's highest decoration, the Congressional Medal of Honor for his selfless acts in the mountains that day.

A movie and a book, *Lone Survivor* had been made about these men. The one surviving Navy SEAL from this mission was Marcus Luttrell and he was standing behind me.

When his eyes locked on the names of his friends on this wall he lightly hit me on the shoulder and uttered the words, 'That's some good shit.'

The wall is 56 feet long and 8 feet high. It's mostly solid black with a dry erase surface that resembles marble to the quick glance of an eye. On this erasable black surface, there are 2,392 small boxes neatly spaced down the wall.

Each small box awaits the name of a hero.

Not an Everyday Hero, as in this book, but in another sense. That is exactly what they are - 2,392 **Everyday Heroes...every day!**

Moms, dads, sons, daughters, classmates and friends.

These are the men and women who wore the cloth of the United States military in Afghanistan and paid the ultimate sacrifice.

The wall resembles the Vietnam Wall in appearance and spirit. The difference being the names were from a war forty+ years later and they are written out from memory each time the wall is displayed.

I'm a veteran of the war in Afghanistan. I joined the United States Navy as a reservist after September 11th and served 2002-2010.

I was 29 years old attending boot camp and had been in my civilian career of teaching memory training seminars for over a decade. Yet, when the Twin Towers fell I knew it was my time.

My grandfather served in World War II in the Pacific and my dad in the Army in the late 60s-early 70s. Make no mistake. This was my time and I knew it.

It was one weekend a month and two weeks in the summer for me for 8 years. With one exception in 2007. That year, I served a deployment to Afghanistan.

When I returned, I continued my career of teaching memory training and I entered and won the USA Memory Championship, breaking the record for the fastest to memorize a deck of cards in the USA at 1 minute 27 seconds.

My card record stood for two years and then I lost my title of USA Memory Champion in March 2011 to the new champ. I stumbled around mentally for the next 8 months contemplating my next move and then one day, looking at the Vietnam Wall with friends, the question was asked, 'How long would it take you to memorize the Vietnam Wall?'

I gave a guess of 4-5 weeks or so for the nearly 58,000 names. It was a bold guess and not even close to the reality I would later discover.

Then it hit me, "Why should I memorize the Vietnam Wall?" I served in Afghanistan. That was my war. My mission soon became clear and I printed out the names of everyone who died in Afghanistan.

Do I memorize them in alphabetical order? That would certainly make it less difficult, because if you got stuck at least you would know you are on the C's, M's or whatever. But no. It's not as symbolic as the order of their death.

Do I memorize just their names (first and last)? With no rank? That would make it a little easier. No. They earned their rank. A military wall must have ranks.

Maybe I could only do rank and last name. No. If I'm going to do this I have to do it the right way.

RANK, FIRST NAME, LAST NAME

It's nearly 7,000 words and over the next 10 months I carried the names of these every day heroes in a black 3-ring binder with me everywhere as I committed them to memory.

I did my best to focus on the task of memorizing names and instead of getting to know the stories. I was afraid if I got too involved in learning the stories, then the emotion of that would distract me from the daunting task of memorizing 7,000 words in sequence.

It was an intense 10 months as I gained 20lbs, didn't shave for months and my every waking thought was consumed with these names, these "everyday heroes."

I would fall asleep thinking of them and my first thought each morning would be of the names. But that is all they were - names. Then February 28, 2013 arrived.

It was D-Day. My D-Day. The day I had set aside to display and perform the wall for the first time. Although I had 10 months of preparation and practice I had never once written the (about 2,200 at the time) names out from start to finish from memory.

I set up the wall at 6am and by 7:30am I was writing the names. My mom, dad, friends and the local media had gathered to witness this task. And I began…

MSG Evander Andrews

Spc Jon Edmunds

PFC Christopher Stonesifer

And on…

I knew the names of some of the heroes on the wall because I had heard their stories.

CIA Johnny Mike Spann was the first US casualty in that country and I knew his story. Michael Murphy, Danny Dietz and Axelson were names I knew because I had read the book Lone Survivor while in Afghanistan, and I knew the stories of a few scattered others. But on this day I began to meet the families on a journey that has changed my life.

1LT Timothy Steele's sister emailed me and explained her brother was killed when he walked across a bridge. One of his men was supposed to go, but was having trouble unlocking his weapon and so Timothy went ahead and stepped on an explosive device.

As I wrote February 28, 2013, I heard the name Austin Staggs from the crowd that had gathered. The local radio and TV were talking about the wall and it was drawing people out from all over the metroplex like metal shavings to a magnet. I turned and asked, 'Ma'am do you know Austin Staggs?'

She replied, 'He is my grandson.'

This grandmother waited for four hours for me to write her grandson's name. I later met his mom and she told me the story how he had only been in Afghanistan a short time when his unit went to meet with ANA (Afghanistan National Army). They stepped out of their vehicles and an ANA soldier opened fire on Austin and five other US military who were killed.

Later that same day, I met Jack Beauchamp the father of HM2 Clayton Beauchamp. Clayton had been a childhood friend of Austin's and when he heard of his friend's death, he enlisted. Clayton also lost his life.

Towards the end of the day, a 30-something athletically built man in business casual clothing was standing motionless at the wall in a fixed gaze.

I continued to write as I felt his presence, just feet from me. I turned to him after 5 or 10 minutes and said, 'Sir, did you know a name on the wall?'

He pointed to Lance Corporal Cody Childers' name and said, 'He was a Lieutenant.' I looked at the name to see if I had made an error and replied, 'I'm pretty sure he was a Lance Corporal.' He then said again, 'He was a Lieutenant.' I closed my eyes and retraced my memory coming once again to the same conclusion and I restated, 'I'm pretty sure he was a Lance Corporal.'

It was only then did he raise his quiet voice and lock eyes with me as he slowly and sternly instructed me with red eyes and pointing to his chest, 'I WAS HIS LIEUTENANT.'

The gravity of what he was saying hit me all at once. I sat back in my chair, nodded my head and turned my attention once again to the wall.

Over the last several years I've written this wall out over 20 times from memory. Each time I have heard stories of heroism and valor from everyday Americans. At one writing, a woman in tears explained to me that her brother was a little guy and so a larger man would carry his backpack on marches and walk ahead of her brother. It was this act that cost the larger man his life as he stepped on an IED but her brother was spared and lived because of this man.

She was in tears as she told the story and I got so caught up in the story I didn't pay attention to the name of the everyday hero. The next day I was so frustrated that I didn't know his name. Then it hit me. It doesn't matter that I don't know his name. This is the story of all the everyday heroes on this wall. They all carried out backpacks. They all went before us. They all gave their lives so we could live. This is the story of the Afghanistan Memory Wall and the 2,392 everyday heroes.

What was my inspiration for the wall? Many things. But one was a regular guy - a bartender at a local bar. This bar had three bartenders. A stylish, fashionable 20-something who hit the gym 4-5 times a week as he meticulously worked to sculpt his appearance and his 20-something female carbon copy counterpart who was equally proud of herself. They both bounced around the bar as if they were the coolest humans to ever grace the planet, full of themselves with condescending glances at anyone who didn't fit their mold of 'hip'.

Then there was another bartender. A humble man who quietly did his job with politeness, kindness, and diligence. It wasn't until I shook his hand one day did I notice he had 3 fingers, and it wasn't until he explained to me about his eye did I realize it was a glass eye. I met his girlfriend shortly after and she disclosed to me that he was an Iraq war veteran and the only surviving member of an IED that hit his convoy.

He's a hero, but if you asked his fellow bartenders they may not even know or, in reality, even care. They are the center of their universe. The Afghanistan Memory Wall serves as a reminder to our nation that the heroes aren't always in the spotlight, they don't always get the attention, might not be defined as hip or cool and their act may have been something as simple as walking into a Navy recruiting office post 9-11 or walking ahead of the other men. But they are heroes, everyday heroes and it is my life's highest dedication to honor them.

The nation that forgets its heroes will also soon be forgotten.

Ron White is a 2 time USA Memory Champion. He is on the National Geographic show Brain Games, History Channel's Stan Lee's Superhumans, the Fox TV show Superhuman with Mike Tyson and Kal Penn and several others. He held the record for the fastest to memorize a deck of cards in the USA at 1 minute 27 seconds and the most numbers memorized in the USA at 167 consecutive digits in 5 minutes. He served in the United States Navy 2002-2010 and was deployed to Afghanistan in 2007. He travels the world teaching his program Black Belt Memory where he takes regular people with regular memory capability and teaches them to be Black Belts in Memory routinely memorizing 50 names in 15 minutes, what they read, foreign languages, speeches, poems, quotes, numbers and more. www.ronwhitetraining.com

ENTREPRENEUR'S WIFE'S JOURNEY

AMY STEFANIK

During the 15 years of living the journey of an Entrepreneur's wife, my faith has been put into question more times than I can count. I've had to face my ego, and I've questioned my purpose. We do not 'find ourselves' on the mountain peaks, we find ourselves in the darkest valleys. Our ego tells us, "I got this." I had to get to a place where my inner light was brighter than my ego.

The problem with being pushed around by the loving hands of the universe is you can let yourself be hardened. When my husband, Matt Stefanik, and I started this journey together, I, had big dreams too. I ventured out in belief and started my own business. When the real estate market crashed, and we lost Matt's business, three houses, our cars, and any sense of security, I also gave up my business and my dreams. With a fall like that, it is easy to be scared to step outside the box again. So I didn't. I played it safe, got a job, created a career in the corporate world, and silenced the voice pleading with me to keep going.

Fast forward to six years later...Matt rebuilt his empire, and we climbed out of the ruins and back to financial freedom again. But the wounds were still there. The injuries created a fear so deep inside me, I was paralyzed. I wasn't living up to my potential; I wasn't listening to that small voice inside me trying to get me to move and answer my calling. We were so busy trying to get Matt's vision off the ground, I stopped listening to that still small voice. When you ignore the universe, bad things can happen. For me, I got sick - not coughing, fever sick - but mentally I was not my best self. Because hurt and resentment took root, I stopped believing in what could be; I ceased to dream.

In fact, the thought of what-if's made me want to cringe.

Matt and I use to look at large multi-million dollar homes to dream, and we would talk about what we wanted to do in the future. But now, I no longer wanted to play the fantasy game. What was the point? I had such a negative dialogue playing in my head, I had no time for dreaming.

My lack of desire to think big was so frustrating to Matt; he saw me disappearing, the light inside me getting dim, and he would try in the best way he knew to reach me, but nothing worked. Our paths were dividing. He felt like I didn't believe in him anymore. We would have arguments about how I was one of his "haters." He would tell me that if I didn't solve this problem now that it would be an issue down the road when he was uber successful. Do you see how the mindset had shifted? It was him, and what he was doing. It was us against each other, instead of us against the world. The war to climb to the top and be successful was nothing like the battle we faced climbing our way back to each other.

The separation we felt was very painful because I wasn't a hater. I was hurting, and I wasn't feeling fulfilled. I was giving and giving, but I wasn't replenishing my tank. Sean Stephenson spoke at an event and said you can develop stuck energy. When we have stuck energy, we lash out and react in negative ways to get this energy out of us. Lashing out could be yelling, drinking, drugs, and other self-destructive behaviors. I chose to shut down emotionally as a way of self-preservation.

This revelation of stuck energy was one of my many 'ah-ha' moments on this journey. I would get so upset and not even know why. I was uncomfortable in my skin. I now know it was my stuck energy. The feeling of being unfulfilled in my life was eating me up. Seeing Matt's success didn't make me mad at him or resentful of him or his success, it made me angry because I was facing my disappointments and lack of personal success.

This battle went on for several years. The lack of communication and the lack of giving on both sides grew into an ugly monster. I had an incredible career; I was a super successful corporate girl. Matt's businesses were flourishing. He was making six figures, but we, as a couple, were miserable. To be honest; this was another crossroad for us. This road was different, though. The decision that we had to make now was, "Will we stay together or go our separate ways?" The anger, resentment, and frustration that we had towards each other almost tore us apart. We are so blessed that God intervened in our lives and said, "That's enough, children!" We believe God put us together and we are destined for greatness. The very dark season of separation that we had to endure made us remember this. It also made us appreciate each other and learn how to give and communicate.

Sometimes you have to be completely broken and humbled to the point of falling on your knees, before God can build you back up and set you on the path again with a new perspective, respect, and outlook on life.

As entrepreneurial families, we are at times so focused on the success, the power, and the lifestyle, we forget how much attention a healthy household requires. The business is not the only thing that needs developing. If you work 24 hours a day and put all your efforts into the hustle, you will probably become very successful. What is success though, if you turn around at the finish line and your family unit is no longer there, if they have become a casualty of the grind.

The "wow" marriage, of course, comes with time, bumps, and bruises. We did not start out this way. That is why I feel the same way when people say, "Your marriage is incredible - you're so lucky!" as I do when people say, "Must be nice!" when they see the fruits of our success.

I believe it's easy to hustle and grind for our business, but leave our marriage - well,- -lacking. We refuse to give up on our dreams but quickly walk away from our marital commitments. We are loyal to our business partners and customers but lack the moral values of being faithful to our spouse. Our lives become very one-sided and self-driven, and when that happens, a profound imbalance occurs. It's hard to be entirely successful when parts of our lives are falling apart. You can hide it for a while; but eventually, it comes out.

Sometimes it is tough. It hurts and feels difficult to be selfless. But if you treat your marriage with the same enthusiasm, dedication, curiosity, belief, and hustle that you dedicate to your business, then your relationship will be unstoppable.

It's sad that we accept the social norm that marriage is not forever. We have let ourselves believe that failing in our relationship has no effect on our business. I do not believe this to be so. I think if you're not getting what you need in your home it is your responsibility to give it the same attention you would if your numbers were plummeting in your business.

We brag about being different, being an entrepreneur, thinking outside of the box, never giving up on our dreams. I think there should be more bragging about having a happy marriage.

Loving your work is a gift, loving your work also makes it easy to neglect other parts of your life. As an entrepreneur, we decide where our time goes.

I'm not portraying perfection. In no way are Matt, and I perfect. We've been beaten up on this journey. We faced divorce because of the lack of understanding and the desire to bend our egos. So no, perfection is not what I'm portraying. I believe we went through hell so we could help others going through some of the same things we battled.

Today I write, coach, lead and teach about hard work, positive mindsets, and always being a work in progress. The journey is not for the weak, but together it is easier to bear. Remember - you are a team! *One Shared Vision*™

 **Amy Stefanik** is a wife, mother, writer, and along with her husband Matt, has been riding the entrepreneur roller coaster since 2002. Amy is the Creator of *The Entrepreneur's Wife*™, whose aim is to help strengthen and encourage the entrepreneurial family. Through *The Entrepreneur's Wife*™, Amy coaches the concept of "one shared vision" in regards to the entrepreneurial journey. Amy is the Co-founder of **GYMRATED**™, an ecommerce fitness apparel and accessories brand, and the Co-founder of **Visentials**, an innovative supplement company.

Entrepreneurs have good intentions, but at times are self-consumed and have very little mental space for anything that is going on around them. This will, at times, include youThe entrepreneur's wife's role is crucial in the entrepreneurial journey. Together you can build an unstoppable empire.

21 Happiness and Success Secrets that Will Change Your Life

Ron Douglas

In a world where money is commonly the scoreboard for success, it's no wonder so many successful people are unhappy. I would argue that you're not truly a success unless you're living a happy life as well. The two do not have to be mutually exclusive if you understand that your happiness is based on your own expectations and can be controlled.

The following 21 happiness and success secrets took me over a decade to learn and compile. They are based on my personal experience on my journey toward achieving happiness. Today I can say that I am truly happy with my life and cherish every day that I get to spend with people I love. I'm extremely grateful for the lessons I've learned and it's an honor to pass them on to you.

1) Choose to be in a good mood Is it possible to choose to be in a good mood? I think it is. It's all in how you perceive things and the things you say to yourself.

For example, a negative person will look at this picture outside of my front door and think it's a rainy, gloomy, winter day. The leaves have fallen, the grass isn't growing, and it's cold out. "This is so depressing. When is Spring going to come?"

A positive person will see the beauty in this picture. The changing of the season is amazing to experience. The beautiful view of the town I have off the side of the hill now that the leaves have fallen. It's a little cold, but not freezing. It's a little rainy but not pouring. The kids are off today and we can have some fun. I feel great.

You can choose how you experience life. I prefer to be in a good mood. You?

2) Be true to yourself Live your dream, not someone else's. Do big things that make you and your loved ones happy, not impress your peers. Examine your goals and why you work so hard. Is it a goal that is 100% true to you, or is it to someone else's dream?

There is nothing like the liberating feeling when you're passionate about what you do and it's consistent with striving towards your dream.

Now, there is nothing wrong with buying expensive things if it's truly your dream. You only live once. But make sure the reason you're doing it is authentic.

Personally, I've never been into fancy sports cars. I'm not into diamonds, expensive art, or flashy stuff. However, my thing is real estate. I want to own lots of property and I want those properties to pay for one big, beautiful property that I live in. My other love is travelling and fine dining. Those are things I'm willing to spend for because they're part of my authentic personal dreams.

On the flip side, my passion is financial freedom and helping others attain it as well. I want to do what I want, when I want, with whom I want, without worrying about money. And I want this for everyone who believes in me and is willing to invest in themselves. So all time spent on that passion is not work, it's love.

Have you clearly defined these things for yourself?

What is your authentic personal dream and what is your passion to get you there?

Please don't go another year without figuring this out. You'll be much happier if you self-evaluate and determine it now, so you already have it in place going forward.

3) Have big goals, but don't focus on goals Have big goals and revisit them often, but don't focus on goals. Instead, focus on the rewards you will enjoy from reaching those goals. Focus on how much better life will be for you and others. Focus on the impact reaching those goals will make. Don't sell yourself the steak, sell yourself the sizzle and it will be easier to keep motivated.

You want to make 7-figures - why?

You want to do a big product launch - why?

You want to build recurring income - why?

You want to develop a SAAS that everyone will use - why?

You want to lose 20 pounds - why?

You want to write a book - why?

Without a clear vision of why, those goals are not meaningful and you're less likely to achieve them.

4) Learn to appreciate the chase We humans used to hunt for food. The adrenaline rush from the chase was necessary for survival. After catching the food, there was an initial satisfaction that eventually wore off, and the next chase began.

Interestingly, that same concept applies to most goals in life. The excitement is in the chase, so we get complacent and take for granted things we've already caught. No adrenaline rush from that, no excitement - just what we become accustomed to having.

Enlightenment is found in being cognizant of this inherent tendency and learning to appreciate the things we have. But equally as important is learning to appreciate how exciting and energizing 'the chase' can be without complaining about the grind required to obtain what you're chasing.

5) Don't dim your light for anyone Ever notice how people love to hear stories of your struggles? It gives them something they can relate to. It makes them feel better about their life. Having those ongoing stories to tell feels good, so people subconsciously tend to stay in struggle mode because stories of wealth and abundance make people feel uneasy about their own situation.

You can feel the negative energy in the little things they say like "it must be nice being you." As if you were lucky and didn't earn it. As if you didn't work your tail off to come up.

You come to realize that it's more socially comfortable just being like everyone else. If you ever wondered how people can hit the lotto and be broke again in a few years, now you know. And to all that I say - snap out of it! You owe it to your loved ones to strive to be the best you that you can be.

Be the exception. Make them feel so uncomfortable that they get inspired enough by you to do something positive with their life as well. Or get new friends. Let your light shine bright and don't dim it for anyone.

6) Do it right now, don't wait That thing you know you should be doing - do it right now, don't wait. You know what it is. Write it down and do it.

Discipline is just making a habit of doing the stuff you know you should over and over. Accomplishing the little things programs your mind to execute the big things. Little stuff done successfully day after day makes you powerful.

Get up and make your bed.

Do 50 push-ups first thing in the morning.

Write an article for your blog.

Prep healthy meals for the day instead of eating out.

Take the steps instead of the elevator.

Contact that person who can help you.

Whatever it is that you know you should do, do it. Practice putting your thoughts into action, consistently. Train yourself to do what you know you should without coming up with a reason not to. Condition yourself to be happy when stuff gets done and disappointed when it doesn't. Learn to embrace your state of flow - that time when you're in the production zone.

Don't underestimate how powerful this is. Once taking action becomes a habit, you can't help but succeed. What's that one thing you should be doing right now? Get in the zone and knock it out.

7) Focus long enough to succeed The easiest thing to do is often the most difficult thing to do. And that is, focusing on one thing long enough to make it work.

Obviously it's easier than trying to do multiple things, but it takes a lot of confidence in that one thing to give it the energy it needs to be successful.

You have to be committed to it enough to not focus on other things, but in the back of your mind there's that fear of failure that makes you think "what if this thing doesn't work?"

So instead of focusing on making it work, it's more comfortable to not be committed to just one thing. Thus, you see people say "I tried that and it didn't work" or "it wasn't for me." But the question is - did you really?

8) Your success level is whatever you settle for Success has a direct correlation with your own self perception and what you believe is acceptable. Deep down, where you are right now is what you deem to be 'good enough' for now. If you really believed that your current situation was unacceptable, you would take action and do everything in your power to change it.

If you want to increase your income, interact with people who are making a lot more than you until what you're earning is no longer acceptable. Become so embarrassed by mediocrity and underachievement that you run out of valid reasons to justify it to yourself. Then your mind will work to envision another level that you must attain and you will do what you have to do to get there. Or you can just be happy and not change a darn thing. That works too.

9) Understand this and get more done You know what you should be doing, so why doesn't it get done? The gap between knowing what you need to do and actually doing it is only bridged by an obsessive desire for change.

If you find yourself procrastinating and not getting things done, it's simply because you don't have to. Subconsciously you're comfortable with where you are right now and changing your routine is uncomfortable.

Change will only come once you're convinced that staying with your current routine is uncomfortable and your present situation is unacceptable. Unfortunately, most people have to hit rock bottom for this to happen.

One of the best ways to break this pattern of self-imposed inaction is to surround yourself with people who are achieving what you want to achieve. People who are driven and motivated by goals instead of despair.

10) Design your ideal life and strive towards it Life is too short not to plan and design it the way you want it to be. You can either take what life gives you and make excuses or you can dictate how you want your life to be and fight to make it so. And even if you don't get exactly what you want, at least you'll have no regrets.

The first step is to be clear on what you want, though. Most people don't even get that far. I'm not talking about material crap like cars and big houses and such. I'm talking about how you experience life and how you spend the one thing you can't get back - your time.

You have to envision what your ideal lifestyle would be:

What would your day be like?

Where would you live?

What would you eat?

Who would you spend your time with?

What would you do for money?

What would do for fun?

What would you do that has meaning for yourself and others?

What would you do independent of the expectations of society and other people?

Once you have these questions answered, then you can develop a plan to get there. Have you ever thought about this?

11) Stress less and earn more What if I told you, you have a better chance of reaching your goals if you're not all stressed out about reaching them?...

Money is a major source of stress for a lot of people. It's a common reason why couples get divorced and families get torn apart. People use it as an indicator of their own self-worth and some even take their own lives if they can't live up to certain financial expectations.

Many people sacrifice their whole life chasing money only to go to their graves with deep regret wishing they had lived a more fulfilling life. Right now many of my friends are probably scrambling to meet some lofty end of the year goal just to keep up with their peers and fulfill their own misguided expectations. "Dang, there's only 3 1/2 months left," as if Dec 31st is some kind of magical deadline day that is any different than any other day. And what's crazy about it is, beyond having food, water, and shelter, it's all B.S.

Time is way more important than money every day of the week. Everything else is just smoke and mirrors and no reason to sacrifice the best years of your life, get all stressed out, and let money affect your health and relationships. Chill the heck out, man.

The truth is, once you learn how to create your own income whenever you need to, you no longer have to worry about money. It matters less how much you make, only that you can make more than you need when you need to. The only thing more liberating than knowing you can create your own income without depending on anyone else is knowing that the income you've already created is out there bringing you enough income to never have to worry about income.

Read that again. That is the one thing I wish I could teach all my friends. If only I could plug a program into the back of your head and upload everything I know into your brain like in the Matrix.

12) Don't knock it until you try it One often overlooked but significant self-limiting habit is our tendency to convince ourselves that something won't work without trying it and giving it a chance.

Our fear of missing opportunities is pacified by telling ourselves things like "he got lucky but that won't work for me" or "nobody really makes money doing that." However, those beliefs are often baseless excuses preventing us from stepping out of our comfort zone and achieving life changing results.

The truth is, your beliefs have gotten you only as far as you are right now. To get to another level, you might have to be thirsty enough to drink the damn kool-aid and try something new. It's sad to see people complaining about their life but refusing to walk down a new path, especially when the footprints of successful people are right there in front of them.

13) Your hidden superpower Do you have a superpower that you're not using?

Our most precious depreciating asset is time and one of our great superpowers is the ability to adapt and form habits over time. The more you master this discipline, the more powerful you become.

They say it takes three weeks to form a habit - good or bad. But it often takes pain or fear to break comfortable old habits and form new ones. For instance, my dentist recently scared the bejesus out of me telling me I need to floss daily to prevent the decay of the bones that hold my teeth in place. I never had a dentist explain it like that. I started flossing everyday and it was annoying at first. Now after several weeks it's a habit and I don't feel right if I go to bed without flossing.

The same thing applies to fitness. When I first started riding my bicycle, it was a pain just to do a mile in the hilly area where I live. But over time, I gradually went farther and farther, and it got easier. Now I can do 10 miles like it's nothing.

What about money or business? Can you get into a habit of saving and investing? Can you get into a habit of networking daily? Can you get into a habit of communicating with potential customers daily? Can you get into a habit of creating? Yes you can. You can adapt. It is your superpower.

The problem is, right now you can't envision just how successful you can be by consistently doing successful things everyday. You can't see that prize at the end just waiting for you. Let me assure you my friend, it is there. Just stop thinking about doing stuff and go ahead and do it. Time is your ally if you use it. It's just math - if you do just 3 things daily, you'll have 90 things done at the end of the month.

Step out of your comfort zone, take action, gradually adapt, form new habits, and use time to your benefit. Most things worth accomplishing are uncomfortable at first. Remember this the next time you think about quitting.

14) Help them help you Success can be simplified to just people making decisions that affect other people's lives. They decide whether they want to work with you, buy from you, do deals with you, have a relationship with you, learn from you, hire you, invest in you, use your talents to achieve their goals etc.

Just people making decisions about other people. Regular people like you and I - one pants leg at a time.

Think about any successful person you know and the same truth applies. If you really think about it, that's all it is. It seems so simple in those terms, however... It is your job to make those decisions easy for them. It is your job to put yourself in a position where the decisions are being made and have the potential to change your life. And it is your job to not give up when the decision is no, because it often will be, but so freakin' what! Keep believing, keep learning, and keep taking steps forward and inevitably it will be yes.

15) Control how you experience life   I believe that God/The Universe gives you signals that you need to heed. Sometimes an event that seems unfortunate is actually a blessing that you shouldn't even question. The saying "everything happens for a reason" is very real. Adopting this belief gives you a completely different perspective on life. You start to realize that everything is happening the way it is suppose to happen and you have faith that things will work out for the best. This kind of optimism attracts only positive things into your life because even when they seem negative, it's only a temporary obstacle on your road to happier times.

I realized this today as we were on our way to a restaurant after Church and hit a pothole that busted a tire and threw off the alignment. It's probably going to cost $150 for the tire and another $100 for the alignment. All in just 2 seconds from one little pothole that I neglected to dodge.

I should really be upset. However, maybe that incident happened for a reason. Maybe we weren't supposed to travel to that restaurant. Maybe we would have gotten into an accident or something.

The point is, don't question when seemingly bad things happen, and don't let them get you down. It's all part of His plan and you're going to be all right. You have the power to control how you experience life.

16) Experience life better   Fortunate is he who can gain old man wisdom while still in his youth. One thing I've learned is you can control how you experience life if you're cognizant of that fact and actually apply it to real world situations.

For example, do you feel rushed when you're in the airport security line?

Do you rush to take off your shoes and try to get all your stuff on the belt quickly so that you don't piss off the other people in line or get scolded by the TSA line police?

I used to do that too until I really thought about why I was feeling pressured and how I could experience life better in this regard. I realized how silly it is to let this social pressure make me feel rushed just to get to the metal detector 14 seconds faster. Now, I'm cool as an 80 year old pimp with a one way ticket to cashville. I get real zen like and take my time and surprisingly nobody gets upset at me. I didn't even have to use my AK, I gotta say it was a good day lol. So I guess what I'm saying is - make a point to experience life better and you'd be surprised at how much happier you'll become.

17) Opportunity favors action Opportunity will not come to you, ever. You can't wish for it, you can't pray for it, and you can't expect others to bring it to you. Opportunity presents itself when you're moving towards it. When you prove that you want it and are willing to sacrifice for it, then magically, it appears.

18) Life is better when striving towards goals Life is much more fulfilling when you have a specific goal you're focused on. The very act of having a goal and a dedicated plan to achieve it gives life purpose and meaning. It gives you a reason to get out of bed energized each day.

Here's how you can improve your life right now - think about what you really want and write down a goal and a plan for getting it. The goal has to have a specific timeframe and be quantifiable.

For example - lose 20 pounds by Jan 1. Get 10 new clients before Christmas. Write 20 pages a week and publish a book in the next 90 days, etc. Once you write it, you have to commit to doing it and refuse to let yourself down. Try this today and tomorrow you will wake up feeling more driven and excited about life.

19) Your expectations determine your happiness

Expectations are such a powerful factor in determining one's happiness. They can either motivate you or make you depressed. Expectations of material wealth, expectations of status, expectations of relationships, etc. Gratitude and perspective are your ammunition against your seemingly failed expectations getting the best of you and stealing your joy.

20) Stress relief exercise If you're feeling stressed - do this now:

Get 4 legal pads and a pen.

On separate pads, write out your things to do, fears, accomplishments, and goals. Keep writing for each topic until you can't think of anything else.

You will be surprised how much better you feel. Rebooting your brain this way helps to get things off your mind and lets you focus. Just give it a try and you'll see how powerful this exercise is.

21) You do what you have to do If someone gave you the exact plan of action that will improve your life forever in the next 90 days, 99% of people would not even attempt it. Here's why:

- You don't have to. People take action when their back is against the wall and they have no choice. The flip side of "you do what you gotta do" is "you don't do what you don't have to do." For most people, having a choice makes their excuses more of a motivator than their reasons why.

- You won't believe it's possible. Either you won't believe that YOU can do it (self-confidence) or you won't believe it can be done at all (socialization). It's amazing that some people can see it being done all around them but still not believe it's possible.

- It will be out of your comfort zone. Most things worth accomplishing in life require you to change and grow and do something you're not accustomed to. Doing the same things will get you the same results only.

- It will require risk you don't want to take. Not necessarily financial risk, but risk of being judged. "What if it doesn't work, what will people say about me?" Most people don't really want you to succeed and get to the next level because it makes them feel insecure about themselves. They'll be rooting you on to your face but secretly wishing you fail so that they have confirmation that they did the right thing by not attempting to do anything. "I told you that crazy thing wouldn't work. Just stick with your job and you'll be all right."

- It won't work at first and you will quit after the first major obstacle or challenge. Life has a way of forcing you to fail before you succeed. You have to take a loss to learn how to win. It's almost as if it's some kind of twisted rite of passage required by the universe.

You will fall flat on your face at times and if you get up and continue, you are closer than ever to achieving your dreams. So it's my hope that this comes at the right time for you. If you're unhappy or dissatisfied with your current situation, do something to change it.

I hope these happiness and success secrets serve you as well as they have me from this day forward.

To your success,

Ron

Ron Douglas is a NY Times Best Selling Author who has been featured live on Good Morning America, Home Shopping Network, Fox and Friends, NBC News, and in People Magazine and has sold over 1.5 million books.

Ron holds an MBA in Finance & Investments, is a Chartered Financial Analyst (CFA), and has worked on Wall Street for J.P. Morgan and Citibank. However, in 2007 he left a promising career and 6-figure job to spend more time with his kids. He went on to earn millions in both online marketing and traditional book publishing while working from home.

Today Ron teaches students worldwide his proven strategies for building a lifestyle business that enables you to earn more while working less.

An Immigrant's Journey To Freedom & Fortune

Janak Mehta

Dead End job with no growth potential and a previous layoff was enough. I was sick and tired of being treated by major corporations like a disposable diaper, and I knew it was time to step out on my own. With only three months of severance pay, I decided it was time to create my own financial destiny and start my entrepreneurial journey.

Before I tell you about my entrepreneurial ventures, let me start with my first few years in the US.

I arrived in the States from India with a dream and a computer engineering degree in August 1999. I joined Carnegie Mellon University for Masters in Computer Science, Electrical Engineering, and a Business school. After graduating from the prestigious university, there were several jobs (17 to be exact) to choose from and I chose the Research Scientist position in telecommunications with Bell Communications Research Lab working on third generation wireless networks. I loved wireless technologies and hence it was typical to spend twelve hours a day, along with weekends, at the office. My goal was to pursue a Ph.D. with Columbia University due to an alliance with Bell Communications Research Lab so I could then start my own High-Tech Company. I guess you could say the entrepreneurial bug has always been in me.

I was the model employee and I loved the awards and recognition that it got me. I was making 6 figures. I was on top of the world. I felt like I made it!!! What happened next was something I could not have planned for. The 9/11 attacks shocked the whole world. New York area and stock markets were hit hard and so was my industry – telecommunications.

Suddenly I was thrown in the unemployment market with a million other people in my industry. I realized how corporate America works. When they need you, they roll out red carpet and when they don't need you, you are out. I decided at that time that I would start my own company one day.

But I didn't have enough cash, credit or courage so I started looking for a job. At first I thought it would be easy since I had 17 job offers in 2000! I did not realize that finding a job was going to be so hard. For six months, I searched within the telecommunications industry before changing my focus. I decided to go back to Pittsburgh and work with my professor on a research project while continuing my job search.

Finally, after 13 months, my job search brought me to the automotive capital of the world – Detroit. I was hired into Ford Motor Company in March 2003.

I found love of my life online! It's the best thing that ever happened to me. And after getting a job, I got married and my wife and I would talk about what our futures would look like. We both came from very humble pasts and knew we wanted to make it BIG in our lives. We started learning about real estate investing, and in March 2004 started our real estate investment business. We bought many training programs and joined local real estate investment groups - and jumped in with both feet! Within the first eighteen months of our business we bought & sold $2.4 million worth of properties. My wife managed the business while I was at Ford.

By March 2005 we joined a local real estate mentoring group and became "model mentees." We started helping our mentor and ended up partnering with him to build a real estate investment club and attracted a growing number of members. We had monthly events with well-known speakers who flew in to share their wisdom. When growing the real estate investment club, we used many online marketing strategies to bring in new customers. Within 18 months, we took the club from 0 to 300 members. Unfortunately, the partnership did not last and we branched off on our own.

We had started learning about Internet Marketing from various Internet Marketing experts, and we attended conferences and seminars to soak it all in. We started implementing those strategies and started getting results. One example – We had bought Matt Bacak's Article Marketing system on CD and started implementing his strategies, and then tweaked his strategies to Press Releases. We started getting results in our own real estate business. We then attended Matt's Millionaire Internet Training (MIT) and when we shared with Matt what we are doing, he suggested we start our own PR Writing and Submission company.

That's how PR Easy was born and I quit my job at Ford Motor company in 2007! PR Easy started with creating and submitting online press releases to get first page search engine rankings for clients. We expanded our services to include Content Marketing, Search Engine Optimization, Search Engine Marketing, and Social Media Marketing. Our clients were small business owners who were looking to maximize their internet presence.

In 2008, while we were growing our marketing company, the real estate market crashed and we had to let go of all 18 properties, ended our partnership, and filed for bankruptcy in early 2009! It was the worst time of our lives. We realized we had stretched too thin and it was not a right partnership.

Looking back, it was a crash course in growing up in the entrepreneurial world. It was not easy and I do not recommend this roller-coaster ride for the faint-hearted. I'm glad that I have a wonderful supportive wife who has stood by my side through the thick and thin!

While going through motions of being at rock bottom, we had to re-invent ourselves. We focused on what we knew - Marketing & Hustling. We knew the Internet Marketing and Social Media Marketing world was exciting and had huge potential. So, we started another division of our company called Social Media Michigan -- one of the fastest growing social media training organizations in the Metro Detroit area.

We grew Social Media Michigan to over 500 members and each month we had 80 – 100 people attending our meetings. With that, we started coaching our members and started a local mastermind in Michigan. We streamlined our services and started focusing on Paid Advertising (Google) and organic Social Media Marketing management for our clients.

We got back on our feet and started growing again. This time we were lot more strategic and we had fun along the way. By 2014, we had decided we were going to focus on just ONE THING. We asked ourselves a very important question, "Out of everything we do, what are we really, really, really GOOD at? And answer was Social Media Marketing & Advertising and more importantly - Facebook Advertising and Marketing.

We slowly moved away from training, coaching and other services and now we focus strictly on Paid Advertising (Facebook, Instagram, Google Adwords) and Social Media Marketing. We now help our clients generate new leads, sales and new clients, customers, or patients in their business.

After growing businesses and selling multi-millions of dollars of information products, services and coaching, we moved from Michigan to Scottsdale, AZ and we are now looking to grow our business at an even more rapid pace.

Here are some of the key lessons I have learned so far in my journey of being my own boss:

1. **Take great care of your Clients/Customers:** Client/Customers are your biggest asset in any business. When you genuinely care for your clients and customers; your business will grow and you will sleep better at night!

2. **Make sure you have the right partners:** I have had bitter experiences in partnering and I think one should be careful before deciding to form partnerships. If the other person is not that committed, then it is a matter of time before the partnership ends. One of the reasons my wife and I get along so well is that we bring complementary skills and hence that partnership has been invaluable in achieving our goals.

3. **You are in the business of marketing:** Without marketing, there will be no sales, therefore no business. So always be in control of marketing for the business. You can outsource individual marketing tasks but make sure that you are in charge of marketing strategies for the business.

4. **Invest in being mentored:** Mentorship is very important to get the information and support from the right people who have already succeeded in your field. I do recommend that you become part of two types of mastermind groups. One group should

be from within your industry and the other one from outside the industry. Cross-pollination of ideas is very useful in taking the business to the next level.

5. **Invest In Personal Development:** We have gone through a lot in life. My wife and I have invested (time, money and effort) in growing personally and professionally. We have worked on our relationships, mindset (80% success is related to having a right mindset) and skills. Entrepreneurship is a journey to become the best version of yourself.

I want to end this chapter with my gratitude towards my family, friends, and this country. I believe that you get second chances in very few places in this world and this is one of those places. So, if an immigrant with a dream and determination can make it in this country; you can too!!! Never Give up and Make it Happen!!!

Janak Mehta – known as a Facebook Advertising Ninja and a Paid Advertising Expert; is a passionate Entrepreneur who thrives on serving, consulting and training business owners and organizations on how to get and scale traffic to their website and turn visitors into clients/customers and grow their business.

Janak Mehta is the co-founder of Clients Online (Formally PR Easy), a full service Social Media Marketing & Advertising Agency based in Scottsdale, AZ. Clients Online helps experts, information marketers, and service-based businesses with Facebook Advertising, Google Pay-Per-Click, Social Media Marketing & Paid Advertising Campaigns as well as various other marketing strategies to accomplish business revenue growth.

THE INCREDIBLE POWER OF "BELIEF"

DAVE SEYMOUR

Long before I smashed into the national limelight on the hard-hitting real estate show "Flipping Boston" I had spent 16 years of my life trading time for other people's money. Doing what? I hear you ask. Well I was blessed to be a Firefighter and Paramedic, serving in a very large city just north of Boston.

I have reflected over and over again on how those years really shaped me to be the industry leader that I am today. I learned that being of service to others is the most powerful action anyone can participate in to create amazing opportunity and subsequent wealth. When we focus our outward energy on helping others, the forces of nature reward us.

Remember how good it felt to buy a holiday gift for someone you cared about? That energy is eternal and when harnessed it's unstoppable. The way to use the power of giving is to do it as often and as big as you possibly can. When it comes to charity, though, I insist you be humble. Someone very important to me once said "The definition of true humility is doing something for someone else and keeping your mouth shut about it."

We have all seen the "Gloaters" who parade as being of service, yet seem to make their efforts more important than the recipients they helped. Your motives should be honorable and pure. It is always a good idea to check your motives when it comes time for taking action.

As a firefighter, the motives were clear - yes, I was paid a salary but trust me, no one becomes a firefighter or medic to gain financial freedom. I am proud of the years I served. I was the first one into a situation and the last one out. I understood how critical it was to be prepared and trained. I also found amazing consistency in the execution of a team. Nobody achieves greatness alone. If people say they are a "self-made" *anything,* then they are a fool and a liar. I never entered a burning building alone and I never came out alone. I never made a home beautiful for resale alone and I have been on this amazing journey with truly amazing people who have shown me that together, we are unstoppable.

Commitment and courage are two of the most misused words in today's ever evolving society. If you were not 100% committed to your engine company then someone could F%$@ing die. If you were not able to be courageous when faced with true life-threatening medical situations, then yes, people would die. Courage and commitment are the foundation stones for measurable success. When coupled with action, things begin to progress at a high rate of speed. This ties into the most mediocre effort people export, ACTION. I had to literally go into the fire to exterminate it. You have to literally DO something to create change. I know how rudimentary this all sounds, but how many times have you just flapped your gums and done NOTHING? Be honest, we are all guilty of talk being cheap. When you read this little piece of wisdom and the other insights in this book, you are given the gift of awareness. The reverse is that you can NEVER be unaware again.

"To thine own self be true."

I want to share the power of belief through a true story that I was a part of one very hot summer, probably 15 years ago now. "If you believe, you can achieve." This philosophy seems kind of like witchcraft or Voodoo. Don't push it aside until you reflect on the intensity of childhood.

I was working my regular 7am-5pm shift assigned to Medic 1. We were the first ALS (Advanced Life Support) unit on any life-threatening call in the city. It was HOT (90+ degrees) and the city was hopping. Working in the tougher inner city areas was exactly where I wanted to be. I wasn't interested in slower stations; I always wanted to be in the middle of the shit. Well, this day the shit got real!

We were dispatched to a "three year old male who had fallen from a 3rd story window." No further information was available from dispatch. These are the calls that send you down a dark tunnel if you are not prepared, committed and courageous. I was instantly talking with my partner running all possible scenarios for what we would be walking into. We were a great team and we knew we were solid. We both knew what our roles were and there was never any doubt that each of us would execute.

It is very difficult to not drive like a complete and total lunatic when children are involved in a medical emergency. I became almost laser-focused on the tasks at hand and getting to scene safely was task #1. I don't care how tough you may think you are, but you are only as well as your sickest child. The thought of my own son being in a situation like we were heading towards was terrifying.

We arrived on scene in less than two minutes, and it was chaotic to say the least. Priority number one was obviously locating the child. This, however, was harder than you would imagine. There was a large crowd of emotionally charged people all standing in a driveway alongside a three decker, or three unit building. They were screaming, pointing up to a window and many were hysterically crying. I feared the worst and expected to see a small child deceased on the ground.

I pushed through the group as fast as I could and when I reached the other side of the driveway I found nothing. I was frustrated and confused that no one was giving me any direction or information. My partner was as bewildered as I was and we needed to get some answers fast! I turned back to the crowd I had just muscled through and saw what appeared to be a mother in the middle of the group holding a small boy. I had walked right past them because in my mind I knew there was no way that that was my patient. I WAS WRONG.

As I got closer the mother was holding the child and she was weeping uncontrollably. I realized the child was indeed the victim from the 3rd floor window. I went into full medic mode. Laying the child down and assessing him from head to toe for breaks, bruises, and deformity of any kind. The little guy was completely calm. He was a Hispanic male and neither his English nor my Spanish were good enough to communicate verbally. We did, however, have a very clear understanding. He looked at me as if to say "what is all this fuss about?"

Then it became very clear to me what had happened, I noticed for the first time that my little buddy was wearing a perfect Superman cape. He was also sporting a splendid pair of rain boots. He was Superman and as we all know - the caped crusader can fly. There wasn't a single scratch on this kid, nothing broken or bruised. I returned to the window and noticed the underneath where superman had landed was a fresh 6" bed of mulch. In the mulch were the footprints of our super hero.

Now understand that the idea isn't to jump from windows to test the power of belief but to remember that childlike belief is in all of us. We have been told NO way too many times. We have been led to "You Can't" instead of knowing "You CAN!". When I counsel others on getting and achieving what they want in life, I always tap into the all-consuming emotion of belief.

Matt Bacak is a leader, innovator and unconditional warrior friend.

Dave Seymour

Dave Seymour

The star of "Flipping Boston" A&E.

I Survived And So Can You!

Devon Brown

"This is it!" I said to my agent.

"This is the office space I want to move into!"

The office space was unlike anything I'd imagined. It was PERFECT!

Brand new, 4,500 square feet, and all of the cubicles, desks, chairs, and other pieces of furniture were already included.

It was in one of those fancy office complexes that was sure to impress anyone.

I told my real estate agent to make an offer on the space.

They were asking $7,000/month for the space (with a 5-year lease), so I told him to offer them $6,500/month.

It was early March of 2014 and I'd been looking for an office space ever since my company launched our new "Done-For-You Sales Team" services in January for people involved in network marketing companies.

The idea, in my opinion, was PURE GENIUS.

Am I maybe a little bit biased because it was my idea?

Sure.

But the shit was still genius, if I do say so myself!

The idea was simple.

Network marketers could pay us a flat fee of just $97 a month, and for that, they'd be able to send traffic to a website we gave them.

On that website, a prospect would be able to fill out a form saying that they were interested in joining a business opportunity.

When a prospect would fill out a form requesting a call back, my sales team would call that prospect and put them into the business (aka downline) of the network marketer who was using our service.

Because I'd been involved in the home based business/internet marketing/network marketing industry for years, I had tons of contacts; so I brought my idea to one of the biggest players I knew.

This guy had a huge downline (i.e. group of people underneath him) in one of the hottest network marketing companies around. And, like me, he thought that my phone-sales-center idea would add tons of value to the marketplace!

So we hopped on a conference call with his downline (over 1,600 people) and told them about my new service.

And guess what…

THEY LOVED IT!

45 minutes later we had over 600 people signed up for my service!

You do the math…(or let me do it for you)

600 people x $97 = $58,200

Yup – I'd just made over $58,000 in about 45 minutes!

That was Monday night at 9 P.M.

By time Wednesday rolled around and others heard the news, we had over 900 people who had signed up for our call center services.

Our first month out the gate, my company brought in about $100,000!

I'd found myself a goose that laid golden eggs…and now, it was time to expand!

That's why I was looking for office space; so that my employees and I could stop working from our homes and behave and grow like a "real" company (notice the quotes).

I'd looked at close to a dozen office spaces and didn't find one that really suited what I *thought* my needs were.

Until I came across this space.

I *knew* this was the one.

About a week after we made our bid, the company who owned the property came back to us and said that they didn't quite understand my business model and that they'd need a full business plan before they could finish processing my offer.

So I spent the next three days working on a business plan and got it over to them.

A week later, their answer came back.

DENIED!

So I said to my agent…"I HAVE to have this office! Withdraw our initial offer of $6,500/month, and offer them the full $7,000/month they're asking for."

He did.

And they came back with their answer…"NO!"

But I wasn't going to be denied.

I told my agent to offer them $7,500/month for the space (a full $500/month) more than they were asking.

And once again, their answer was NO!

I was LIVID!

Couldn't they see that I had a $100,000/month tiger by the tail?

Couldn't they see that this office space was supposed to be mine?

"F@CK THEM!" (I thought to myself)

How could this happen to me?

How could God give me a $100,000/month business, show me this great office, and then not let me have it?

30 days later my agent and I settled on a different office space.

The space we finally acquired wasn't nearly as new (or as nice) as the space I'd fallen in love with; but it was much closer to my house (only 10 minutes away as opposed to 25).

This new space was about 2,900 square feet and the cost was about $3,000/month less than half of what the other people wanted). Not to mention the fact that the landlord was willing to do a 3-year lease (as opposed to the 5-year lease I would've had to sign at the other place).

I half-begrudgingly (and half-gratefully) moved into my new space in May of 2014 (a full 90+ days after I'd had my $100,000 month).

So (a quick recap), in January of 2014 I launched my idea and had my first $100,000 month...

In May of 2014 I finally moved into some office space (office space that was smaller and less expensive than what I hoped for and thought I deserved).

Soon after I moved in, my business started going downhill.

I won't get into all of the details, but by September I could barely afford to keep the lights on.

By February of 2015 (less than a year after we moved in), my staff and I were barely working out of the office.

By June of 2015 I was paying $3,000/month for an office that no one was using.

By November of 2015, I was thanking God for allowing me to find someone to subcontract my lease for the final year and a half so that I wouldn't be responsible for the payments anymore.

I was sooo grateful to be out of that lease.

But can you imagine what would've happened had life actually gone the way I'd wanted?

Can you imagine where I'd BE if I'd actually gotten what I asked for?

By the time I was 6 months into my lease, I could barely afford the rent.

Can you imagine how bad it would've been if my rent were literally twice as much?

I wouldn't have survived financially.

Heck, the whole reason I was even able to get someone to sublet from me was because there was only a year and a half left of the lease and the landlord didn't care what I did, as long as the rent was paid... (unlike the landlord at the original space I wanted which was a corporate entity and not an individual).

The morning after all of the sub-leasing paperwork was completed and the company that would be taking over the payments had the keys to the office in hand, I woke up light as a feather. As if a $3,000/month weight had been lifted off of my shoulders.

And as my mind relived the journey I'd been on, and how things would be infinitely worse had life gone my way, it hit me.

As if a little voice had whispered an epiphany in my ear.

An epiphany that made me completely reconsider everything I thought about life, circumstances, and happiness.

"It's not happening <u>TO</u> you… It's happening <u>FOR</u> you!"

That was it.

Those were the 9 words that completely changed everything for me.

I realized that when God, the Universe, or whoever you want to call it was not letting me have that $7,000/month office, that wasn't being done TO me… it was being done FOR me!

Taking out the word "to" and replacing it with "for" made me see my life as if I were looking through glasses that gave me super-vision.

Instantly, my mind started searching for times I didn't get what I wanted - only to show me something better around the corner that I couldn't see before.

I thought about time I was stood up by this girl at a local bar, only to have that be the night I would meet an amazing woman that I would end up dating for over a year and remain great friends with to this day.

I thought about the time that some scam artists infiltrated one of my businesses and ended up making me lose about $8,000 and an entire month's worth of work. As it turns out, the changes I had to make in my business because of these scammers ended up yielding me about $2,700/ month in profits!

I thought about back in highschool when I sang in the choir and tried out for the advanced choir only to fail miserably. I thought life wasn't going my way. I almost quit the choir . But the next year, while "stuck" in the choir I didn't want to be in, I met the guy who would become my best friend. We'd end up going to college together (to a school I'd have never even considered had we not been friends). The four years at Georgia Southern University (where I went to college) and the friendships I made that still shape my life to this day, would've NEVER happened had I gotten what I wanted.

Instance after instance I came to realize that whenever I thought life wasn't going my way, it actually WAS going my way. It was just doing so in a way I couldn't understand at the time

I even started looking at the lives of my friends to see if this same principle held true.

"Life can only be understood looking backwards, but it must be lived forwards." – Soren Kierkegaard

I thought about a female friend of mine who, only a few years earlier, went through a divorce because her husband had cheated on her.

Did she deserve that?

No.

Did she get what she wanted (i.e. a fruitful and faithful marriage with her husband)?

No.

What she got was something 100X better.

The guy she met after her divorce was *exactly* who she was supposed to be with.

They're happily married to this day and I couldn't be happier for her!

But you see…

With regard to her cheating husband, her divorce, and all the rest of that "negative" stuff…

None of it was happening TO her…it was all happening FOR her!

It was happening so that she could get a *bigger* blessing.

I'm not overly religious, but when the bible says *"I will take your ashes and turn them into beauty"*…

I now understand what those words mean.

So, as I close out this commentary, I have two questions I'd like for you to ponder as you go about your day…

Question #1: How many times in your life have you thought something was happening TO you, only later to find out that it was happening FOR you?

And

Question #2: What if the next time life doesn't go your way (or you don't get what you THINK you want) you were to apply this idea that it's happening FOR you instead of TO you?

Try doing this the next time life gives you what you THINK are lemons.

Choose to believe that it's happening FOR you (instead of TO you), and see how excited you get about how your ashes could get turned into beauty.

Devon Brown (a.k.a The Success Renegade)

From bankrupt at the age of 23, to now generating as much as $100,000 a month in his home-based business, Devon Brown has become one of the most talented young success coaches & speaker/motivators for home business entrepreneurs.

His teachings are not only power-packed and filled with laughter; but they also contain simple, practical, & fun illustrations that virtually any entrepreneurially minded person can use to improve the marketing and sales aspects of his businesses.

A student of personal development for well over a decade, Devon makes sure that his clients understand that success is a PROCESS (not an EVENT). And his personal journey from failure to success is one that gives his own students & clients the inspiration they need to succeed.

NEVER SKIP THE STORY

JEANNE KOLENDA

In my 66 years on earth, I have always been drawn into a good story. When I was a child, I made trips to the local library quite often, toting home a shopping bag full of good books. I read under the covers with a flashlight, long after I was supposed to be asleep.

We were poor financially when I was growing up, but rich in so many things – love of music, books, art – and I was loved unconditionally every day of my life. Like I said – RICH! When we didn't have the money to travel, I could go places with a good book; I could close my eyes and "see" the places and "hear" the sounds of voices in my mind. All because of good storytelling.

So, when I became a marketer, it came naturally to tell stories. Not lies, but stories that revealed the history of a business or the fascinating lives of the business owners. Now, I know – some people are just plain boring, but more often than not, an individual has a really good story behind his success. Some folks are just introverts, and the story must be drawn out carefully.

But just think about it – how much more interesting to hear the story of the Italian guy who owns the local pizza and pasta joint, than to just eat the good pizza! What if you knew the history of his parents immigrating to America with nothing but a dream? What if you knew why he chose YOUR community to settle down and raise a family and start a business? What if you knew his stories of failure and loss and perseverance that are the history of that yummy pizza and pasta that you take for granted? What if you knew you were enjoying Uncle Giovanni's secret family recipe that has been safely guarded for over a century? Would you look forward even more to eating there and even recommending it to your friends and family? I think so.

- ➤ Stories communicate
- ➤ Stories sell
- ➤ Stories inspire
- ➤ Stories make a difference
- ➤ Stories leave a legacy

I never build a website for a business without completely understanding the "story" of the business, and finding a way to artfully weave it into a cutting edge marketing strategy. Never skip the story.

Sometimes in the line of marketing I do (hardcore SEO and ranking sites for businesses), I can get lost in the minutiae of the processes required to get results, and lose sight of the power and the beauty of the stories to be uncovered with each business. My writing this chapter will serve as a reminder to me to never let that go on for too long.

What would a chapter on the power of stories be without a story?

When I was in Barcelona, Spain last year, speaking at a marketing conference, I asked the host if I could speak on "half business and half inspiration." He agreed and thought that was a good idea. So, I did the usual introduction – a little about myself, and my business history, and why I was qualified to stand and speak on the subject of business building. And, of course, I told some personal stories of having overcome some major obstacles in my life. These included divorce, death, a heart attack, an accident that left my precious daughter struggling for her life for years, and although she survived, life as we knew it was over. Heartbreak, disappointment, bankruptcy, a trusted business partner who betrayed us. I didn't want anyone getting the notion that I had led some kind of charmed life. But not to worry…I included stories of victory, healing, and how it all has led to a life full of joy and love, and the freedom and flexibility that I always craved.

So, then, I put down my notes, leaned in and said, "Can I tell you a story?" Everyone perked up. And here, I share it with you…

The Sound of Heavy Rain

"In the year 800 B.C., Kings ruled the Middle East. Each King has his special 'prophet, or seer' and when he needed an answer on a subject of importance, he called for the prophet to get an answer from the higher powers. Now, if the prophet received and delivered an answer that wasn't what the King was hoping for, he might kill him. Have you ever heard the saying, "Don't kill me…I'm just the messenger!" This is probably where that originated.

In a certain region, there was a severe drought that had afflicted the land for almost 3 years. In today's world, if we have a drought, we have ways of dealing with it – water has been stored, we can release dams that hold back rivers. In other words, it isn't a matter of life and death. But in 800 B.C. it meant certain death. The king needed an answer. People were dying.

This was a king named Ahab who had a reputation for being harsh. He called for his prophet and sent him away to seek answers to save the lives of the subjects of the kingdom. The prophet did as he was told. He didn't stay gone long; he received his answer quickly. Here's the message he delivered to King Ahab: 'Go ahead – eat, drink and have a party because I HEAR THE SOUND OF HEAVY RAIN!' Seriously? He heard the sound? How did that happen? There wasn't a cloud in the sky and rain was nowhere to be seen. Can we hear rain coming if the skies are sunny? No. I can only assume the prophet 'heard' the rain in his spirit. Something deep inside of his being assured him rain was on the way.

But even a prophet can need some assurance. So, he sent his servant (I like to call him the VA - virtual assistant) out to the edge of the sea to look for a rain cloud – or two. The servant came back after a trip to the sea and reported, 'Sorry, I've got nothing!' Uh-oh. So the servant was sent to the same spot SIX times and came back each time with a bad report – no sign of rain. On the 7th trip, he came back and said, 'I see a cloud the size of a man's hand!' That's all it took for the prophet – he was over the moon excited because he would not be killed by the king for giving a false message. Soon, the rains came and it was a DELUGE! The drought was over.

Here's an important observation from this true story from history…

The servant was sent to the *same* spot to look for the answer. He wasn't sent down to the city, up the mountain, or off to the countryside. It was TO THE SEA each time. The prophet KNEW from where the provision would come. How about you? When you don't quickly see your plans coming together, do you start to look elsewhere? Here's an example: You start off in niche affiliate marketing…that doesn't pan out, so you decide to get into eCom. That's too hard, so why not do local search marketing…or maybe get rich with Kindle publishing of eBooks. I think you get the picture. Pick a plan and FINISH WHAT YOU START, unless there's a very compelling reason to switch gears. After all, any of these ways of making a small (or large) fortune will work if one is prepared, focused, and willing to do the work. You'll just delay the desired result if you keep diluting your efforts by being indecisive about what business model to pursue.

(Long pause…)

How many of you have experienced or are right now experiencing drought in your lives?

In your personal life?

In your marriage?

In your business?

In your soul?

Do you need to hear the SOUND OF HEAVY RAIN?

It's possible, if you keep your heart and your mind in a posture of expectation and faith, always seeking the truth and believing it can happen. Then do the work. Finish what you start."

(At this point in the story, I flashed a huge picture of a heavy rainstorm on the wall).

I asked,

"Do you hear it?"

"Do you hear the rain?"

"DO YOU HEAR THE SOUND OF HEAVY RAIN!!??"

At first it was very quiet, there were even some tears, but then slowly people stood and offered thunderous applause, while they yelled, "YES, we hear it!"

➤ People were touched.

➤ People were inspired.

➤ People were encouraged.

➤ It was the power of the story.

Never skip the story.

Jeanne Kolenda has lived in Myrtle Beach, SC for 27 years. She's been married to Leon for almost 3 decades and together they have 4 children and 6 grandchildren. Jeanne has always made it her plan to do things "out of the box," and homeschooled her kids before it was legal (35 years ago). She's always found a way to earn an income working from home. Sometimes it was successful and sometimes not, but the freedom and flexibility were worth it. For the past 25 years, she and her husband, Leon, have owned and managed an automated answering service, In Touch Solutions, primarily serving the medical community nationwide.

In 2010, Jeanne discovered online marketing, and took to it like the proverbial duck to the water. She has succeeded in helping local "brick and mortar" businesses market their businesses online. To some it's called "offline marketing," but whatever you call it, Jeanne rocks it out for business owners.

Some of her techniques and strategies were so unique, it caught the attention of some of the big players in the info-product and training world, and she was introduced to and coached into creating courses to offer to others who have digital agencies, serving the local business market.

By having folks buy her courses, she developed a following (a list) and now is also involved in some affiliate marketing.

She's 66 years old, and doesn't mind anyone knowing that – in fact, she's "proud to have survived this long!" Retirement isn't in her vocabulary, and her love of learning, communicating, and helping others while developing deep friendships keeps her energized.

She has been an instructor several times at NAMS (Novice to Advanced Marketing Systems), a long-running conference held in Atlanta for years, and a popular speaker at other marketing events. In Fall 2016, she attended a Mastermind in Barcelona, Spain, and delivered a speech to a group of marketers from all over the globe. Much of this Chapter is taken from that talk given in Spain.

Although home is still Myrtle Beach, you'll find Jeanne and Leon, and their Standard Poodle, Andy, out in their RV many months a year, living the Digital Nomad lifestyle.

Jeanne is the Queen of the "F" words.

Most everything important to Jeanne starts with the letter "F":

➤ Faith

➤ Family

➤ Friends

➤ Freedom

➤ Flexibility

Contact Jeanne at jeannekolenda@gmail.com

http://jeannekolenda.com

FB: Jeanne Beemer Kolenda

LEARNING MEASUREMENT TO IMPROVE

PHIL PERRIN

Growing up I have always been interested in how things work and ways of reducing waste. Having trained in statistics and Lean Six Sigma, as a coach / mentor it's very satisfying helping others to improve.

One day in a meeting with some process engineers, they were talking about how many plastic bottles they were throwing away, whilst setting up an induction sealing process. "It takes us at over 600 bottles to get them to seal right," said Gary, the packing manager, and asked if I could help them out.

I responded, "We will need the process engineers, the operators on the line and the design team. Please set up a meeting and get a flip chart then we can capture the problem."

The next day we gathered in the room; there were six of us there - Jane and Sharon who operated the production line; Gary, the packing line manager; Tom, the bottle designer; and Chris, a trainee from the Operational Excellence team.

Prior to the meeting, an agenda was created and Gary was asked to bring along some samples of the problem bottles to illustrate the problem.

The team arrived and the first thing was a quick introduction of who we were and our involvement in the process. The next agenda item was to generate a problem definition.

Gary explained that smaller bottle necks sealed well, but the larger necked bottles always required larger setup runs to make a good seal, which produced loads of scrap. Then he started to go into solution mode. "Hang on Gary... let's hear what the others think, before trying to solve it! Jane what do you think - we always have problems with the larger bottle necks, the speed is critical if it's too slow the seals overheat and if it's too fast they don't seal." Tom verified this was true, but told the group there were other settings that affect the seal, such as input power, current, and height of seal in the tunnel. We also had different card thicknesses on the foil seal and different torque settings that affect the seal as well, added Sharon.

Ok now let's create some problem definitions. Everyone wrote their own problem definition down and read them out, we then voted for the one below by consensus.

"We are currently rejecting 600 plastic bottles setting up the line to seal the 55 mm necks on plastic bottles using an induction sealer. This is costing us $800 per setup. There are several things that affect the sealing including line speed, height in the induction tunnel, power setting, thickness of foil seal plus backing card thickness and torque of the lid."

Do you have a standard operating procedure for this process? We do have a procedure, said Jane, but it has not been updated for a while. Can we see what the settings you use? We record speed, torque and power settings in the process logbook.

Great! If you bring me the logbook, we can review them later. I explained that the process operators are key to improving their processes, because they operate them most of the time, they often notice things that affect the output. Have you noticed anything else that has changed which could affect the setup? We have been using different foils in the lids. The thickness of the packing disk also changed, said Sharon.

Tom explained we have tried a thicker aluminum foil to get a more consistent heating effect - this meant that the packing material needed to be thicker. Did you change anything else? We did adjust the power applied to the induction coils, said Jane.

Chris was busy scribbling notes in his book. What else can vary during the setup? We set the height in the induction tunnel by ruler and eye said Sharon.

Can you fit a spacer in the machine to control the height of the bottles so that the foil seal is at the same height consistently, I asked? Great idea, said Gary but, what height is best? We will need to set up a designed experiment to decide that. That sounds complicated, said Jane, don't worry it's quite simple, we just need to determine which inputs cause the output to vary then set them at different values, and measure the output in some way to determine if the output is better or worse.

The first step we need to create a matrix with the inputs down the left-hand side and the value we want to set them at I suggest we use the maximum and minimum values with a centre value.

The number of runs should be repeated in a random way. Why can't we just set up one run and repeat it again afterwards? Good question, Sharon - the answer is that if a setting is not quite right it will skew the results but, if you reset it a few times you are more likely to spot a trend in the results and you can then repeat the run if necessary. We usually repeat each run several times to get a good idea anyway.

Tom asked we have two different foils could we repeat the experiment for each type to find out which one is better. That will double the number of runs you need to perform but, the answer is yes, in fact, we have quite a few different settings. I suggested we list them out and decide if we can fix any of them at a value, if, in your experience, they don't affect the output.

We have:

1)Torque of lid, 2) Induction Coil Power, 3) Height in Induction Tunnel, 4) Conveyor Speed, 5) Foil Type, 6) Card Packing Material Thickness.

We never change the torque of the lid, said Tom, so we could eliminate that, also the foil type and packing material will be fixed for each type so if we are going to do two experiments for the different foil and card combinations, that leaves us with three factors per experiment.

Sounds good to me, Tom, does everyone else agree? Great! All we need to do now is come up with a measure of the output.

If we undo the lid and squeeze the bottle in a bowl of water you can tell if the lid has sealed by any bubbles escaping, said Gary. If we run 10 bottles per setup we can get a score out of 10 per run for good seals. Sometimes if the foil gets too hot it burns the side of the bottles, said Jane. You can record a second set of results for cosmetic failures, I said. Then, we can determine the best settings to avoid them.

If you can tell me the maximum and minimum settings that you usually use from your logbook I will set up an experimental matrix with Chris for you to run the experiment. Later that afternoon, Sharon brought the log book of settings to me later that afternoon.

Can you can arrange to get 580 bottles, lids, foils and card inserts so that we can start tomorrow? Gary, is there any way we can check the speed of the conveyor? We have a checker that is a wheel that runs on the conveyor and records the speed. Good! Make sure you bring that along...now, what about the height in the induction tunnel - can we make that any easier? I will also get some spacers made up to slide in between the bottle top and the top of the induction tunnel. Excellent! I will set up the experiment with Chris this afternoon and I will see you all at the packing line tomorrow.

Sitting down with Chris we defined the factors and levels with a Maximum and Minimum for each setting and a midpoint at the typical setting used. Then we entered the data into a Stats program that set up an array randomising the run order. There were three factors with two levels with three centre points and three replicates giving 28 runs per experiment.

We entered the values for speed power and height, then let the software create the test array.

Everyone was there at the line. Tim and Gary were eager to get involved and I believe it is best if Jane and Sharon operate the line as they are already experienced.

How long does the conveyor take to get up to speed? Let's test it, said Gary - I have the Gauge.

On measurement, it took 5 seconds to get up to speed. Ok, Sharon set the ten bottles up for the first run back over there before the lid torque process so that the conveyor will be up to speed as the bottles pass through the induction tunnel. Which foil and lid do you want to use first? The thicker one, said Tom.

If you set up the power and conveyor height Jane, Gary has made up some spacers for you to make it easier. That's a lot easier than using a ruler and more repeatable too. Chris will tell you the settings for each run. Tom, will you test the bottles for leaks in the bowl of water and record the score per run.

All set let's start! The power was turned on and the first bottles started moving towards the lid torquing tool, then they moved into the induction tunnel after they had all gone through. Sharon stopped the line everyone was eagerly looking at Tim who was testing - the seals six are good, he said. Ok. Just repeat the runs for the other setups and then repeat for the other foil and packing materials. After about an hour the runs were all completed.

Thanks team! Can we meet back here after lunch so that we can do a confirmation run? Chris and I will analyse the results now.

The analysis of the data showed that a height using a 10mm spacer was best with an interaction between the conveyor speed and power. That's interesting - it doesn't need as much power for the thicker foil, said Chris, and we have two optimums, one for each foil. When we use the best combinations of settings, we don't see any burning. Let's do a confirmation prediction. How do you do that, asked Chris. I showed him a feature of the software that used an analysis of variance technique and explained how that the result should be within 10% of the prediction.

We went back to the packing line that afternoon. Let's try these settings and see what happens, I said.

The team was excited, the result confirmed all ten bottles sealed perfectly for both foil and card combinations. Tom and Gary were amazed. That's fantastic! - we can now set up the line without scrap. That's the power of statistics, my friends! I have taken you through a typical Six Sigma improvement project using four powerful steps. There is one step left, someone needs to write a standard operating procedure for this product with pictures of the setting up process. I will do that this afternoon, volunteered Sharon.

The five steps I have taken you through are Define, Measure, Analyse, Improve and Control.

Later that week, the whole team was taken out for a meal as a thank you for their help, solving the problem, the scrap rate dropped from 600 bottle to zero per setup.

Phil Perrin is a confident, versatile and enthusiastic coach experienced in training developing and leading teams.

Motivating and mentoring business owners to measure and take proactive actions, to increase both profit and growth.

Focus is typically in one of 11 areas: Profit, Cash-flow Marketing, Sales, Strategy, Teams, Innovation, Systems, Teamwork, Operational Excellence and Time Management. Always passionate about helping others, working to the highest standards and creating win-win scenarios. Check out my website at: http://KentBusinessImprovements.org

FROM HOMELESS TO HELPFUL
HOW REINVENTION HAS SHAPED MY LIFE

BRIAN BASILICO

How does it feel living the high life? I am not really sure. I was running a half million dollar business with five employees, working with celebrities, and starting to see years of hard work start to pay off.

I was running a commercial recording studio in the basement of an office complex. The offices were on the first floor and we had two fully functional recording studios and a cassette duplication business in the basement. We had a 16-track studio in one suite for music, with two digital suites for voice overs and commercials. We were proud to be one of the first studios in Chicago to add digital computer-based editing to each studio. We eventually added audio for video synchronization and were one of the first CD production companies as well. The business was flying high and running on all cylinders.

Then came the sh!t storm… literally. The landlord hired a contractor that broke a sewage line and flooded the basement with raw sewage. The business quickly went in the crapper and I was pissed (on). The basement was shut down for 3 months and the downward spiral started.

Eventually we had to relocate to a smaller building and re-build the business. In the process, we lost enough customers that I had to take a day job with another production company to make ends meet and left my employees in charge of the business.

The troops got restless with slow paychecks and started to worry the ship was sinking. I came back one day into the office before closing, and the employees told me they were leaving to start their own company and taking my clients with them. That same day, I received a letter from the IRS that I owed $7000 in back payroll taxes. I was already $75,000 in debt and had no money to pay back-pay or the IRS.

Oh, by the way, I was in the middle of a failing marriage. My wife left me and I was homeless, sleeping on my sister's couch. All that I was left with was a failing business, two boxes of clothes and my guitars.

I continued working the day job and coming in at night to complete projects and handle the bookkeeping. There was one night where I was just so distraught, I stopped at a gas station and picked up a six-pack of beer and a pack of cigarettes. I just sat in my office smoking and drinking trying to figure out how I was going to get out of this mess. I had to shift from the victim mode to owning the situation. I eventually came up with a plan.

The plan included giving equipment to the now past employees in exchange for most of their back pay, and then to sell off enough gear to pay off the IRS.

Eventually, I left the second job and limped through for months. Then one day, I was approached by one of the customers who did not leave, and they wanted to buy my business and give me a job. Guess how much I sold the business for? Yes... $75,000 -- so I was zeroed out!

The lesson learned from this reinvention was that as much as you feel like you control your life, life really controls you. What you can control is your attitude and reactions to the hand you've been dealt. Also, you don't have to go it alone, so always be willing to ask for and accept the help of others!

Act 2

I was finally able to rent a home and get off the couch. This transition became a time of reinvention. Sitting on the porch, I started to explore who I was, how did I get here, and what was next.

It was time to get back to the core of who I really wanted to be. What was my passion? What was my purpose? First off, I was a musician. I had played in bands since I was in junior high until well into my 20's. Even though I would eventually realize that I don't play well in the corporate sandbox, it did give me the freedom to be a connector, a creative, and a collaborator. Running a business with employees turned me into a paper pusher and took me away from creative activities that I loved before growing the business. At my core, helping others succeed was my passion. I went back to the mission statement of that studio: "Your Success Is Our Business!"

Making Music

I was invited to check out a church that met in a movie theater. Eventually, I found myself standing on stage again playing live music. It was quite different than being in a band since you got there at 5:30 am and were back home before noon.

After getting a taste of being a musician again, I decided to join a band. I was accepted with my first audition with 'The Pretzel Boyz'. Although it was fun being with a great group of musicians, it was like a night job (I already had my day gig at the production company). From the time we started loading gear, played for three hours, packed up and unloaded gear, it was an eight-hour adventure every gig. After paying for gear rental, the sound man and more, we were lucky to get paid $50 each (which was enough for a set of strings, gas and maybe a beer at the end of the night).

Two major things came out of the band gig. First, I met my future wife, Kim. She worked with the keyboard player's wife. Second, after the band broke up, the guitar player and lead singer (Mark) and I started an acoustic band called "Dough!" We were the unplugged Pretzel Boyz (and pretzels are made out of dough).

Volunteerism

I stuck with the church as it moved to a high school and ultimately, its own building. The church moved to Aurora, IL, and eventually Kim and I built our house right across the street from the church.

The church became very involved in the community. Soon I was volunteering for the United Way on their marketing committee. Eventually, I was elected to the board of directors and ran the marketing committee for 6 years, and I still work on that committee today.

Because of that partnership, we were able to persuade the church staff to start, and fund, two major initiatives. The staff would spend time and money to see these through for years.

During the summer, we created "Operation Helping Hands." We assembled over 500 volunteers to do project work for one day to help the agencies that the United Way supported. We had teams all over the city doing projects like painting rooms, landscaping, and more. It was a win-win because the agencies could not afford to pay for the project and we could donate the staff and supplies to get projects done that helped them better serve the community. The city eventually got involved donating staff time and tons of mulch and supplies. I coordinated with all of the partner agencies, worked with teams of volunteers and staff to plan the day, and worked alongside families on the day of the projects. This was a very time-consuming venture that took me over 100 hours to coordinate each year.

During the winter, we created "Adopt A Child." At Christmas time, there are many organizations that provide gifts for needy families. We found out that schools in the city were identifying kids and families that had fallen through the cracks. We worked with the schools to identify the needy kids, and then the real work started. We created custom ornaments with the child's age and gender. Church members would line up to choose an ornament and were given a list of the child's needs. They could spend up to $50 per child. Parents loved taking their kids to shop for the gifts to show them just how far that would go. If you bought a coat (the most requested item) you had very little for socks, toys, or whatever. From before Thanksgiving to a week before Christmas, we would distribute ornaments and take delivery of the gifts. At its peak, we served over 500 children. Again, this took over 100 hours to coordinate. I am proud to say that this initiative was taken over by the United Way and continues every year.

The lesson learned through this reinvention was that I needed to evolve from being self-absorbed to becoming self-aware. It taught me the concept of servant leadership. Giving your time, talents, and treasure can create abundance in your life through relationships.

Act 3

Back in 2001, I had my last stint in the corporate world and decided to open my business as a solopreneur. I took what I learned at the agency that bought my business and started programming CD-ROMs, websites, video and more.

It has been a wild ride, to say the least. Over the course of that time, CD-ROMs and DVDs have all but disappeared. Social media started its rise in 2004 and internet marketing was coming into its prime. Over the course of the next 10 years, it was a series of reinvention... for myself and my business.

During that time, I started to learn my true super power. It was teaching, and I loved it. Being a musician, I had no problem standing up and performing in front of crowds. Speaking and presenting feels like performing without a guitar in my hands. One of my favorite quotes is "When you teach... you learn twice!" and that is the truth. I started combining my 30+ years of experience in marketing and relationship building with presentations and teaching. I started getting offers to teach at community colleges and soon was teaching parts of a social media and marketing Masters class at a university.

The most important part of this is that it started to help me organize this information into a cohesive package that people were responding to in very positive and proactive ways. I started to sense a hunger for this information to be organized and packaged for mass consumption.

In 2012, I started writing my first book, *It's Not About You, It's About Bacon! - Relationship Marketing In A Social Media World*. It started out as a social media how-to book, but was obsolete by the time I finished chapter 3 because social media was changing so quickly. That's when I decided to write a why-to book, and that was one of the best decisions I have ever made. The book was completed and launched in 2013 and my life has never been the same.

First off, I never thought of myself as a writer. As of today, I have completed four books and I am working on book number five. I was invited to conferences and have spoken from the stage at most of them. I have met some incredible influencers in the internet marketing and social media space, and many of them have since become friends. I started a popular podcast and used it as a platform to interview those influencers and have met many more in the process. And, I have created a worldwide brand around BACON (which stands for Building Authentic Connections On-line Networking).

Final Thoughts

I hope you can see how this journey helped me to start over and learn that we all have a greater purpose. Mine was to learn that by serving others, you will not only make a difference in the world, but completely change your world. I had to be completely broken down to be built up. I needed to learn to serve others first to learn my own purpose and super power. Finally, I used reinvention as a tool throughout my life to stay current, relevant and purpose-driven.

I am so looking forward to Act 4…

Brian Basilico is an award-winning and internationally recognized author, speaker and online strategist. He's the founder and president of B2b Interactive Marketing Inc., an award-winning marketing consulting and production company in Aurora, Illinois. B2b helps companies and nonprofits market their products and services through the effective use of online tools including; websites, blogs, email, social networking, Google, SEO, YouTube, and more.

Brian's career spans over 35 years. Since starting his first production company in 1979, he's produced thousands of projects for companies ranging from solopreneurs to Fortune 100. Brian combines years of marketing experience with technical expertise to build online campaigns that produce measurable results. As a musician, technician, programmer, producer and consultant, he has built a reputation for creativity, innovation, and translating "geek" into English. Brian is also an adjunct professor, trainer, author of many social networking and marketing blogs, and an avid podcaster. He has been featured in articles in Inc. and Entrepreneur magazines. To learn more about Brian, visit www.b2b-im.com.

RELATIONSHIP RICHES: THE ULTIMATE LEVER FOR MAKING A DIFFERENCE IN THE WORLD

SHERRIE ROSE

Do you want to be liked? I know I do.

It is a deep-rooted desire to be liked and with billions of people on our planet, living in harmony, getting along, and boosting others up, is vital to being effective and happy.

You may want more to be liked. You may want to be popular. Being liked or being popular starts first with liking other people. When you genuinely like other people, in a sincere way, not for a purpose, you will generally be liked in return.

This all seems rudimentary, but it is not always easy. Some people, well, are difficult to like. Liking requires practice and the more you do it, the easier it becomes.

I'd like to share my personal motto: *"The Real Currency is Relationship Riches."* When you first meet another person it may begin as an interaction as a medium for an exchange just like currency changing hands. As the relationship develops, there is a collective experience which goes beyond the 'you scratch my back and I'll scratch yours' transaction. (This idiom was first recorded in 1704.)

Almost 100 years ago, Martin Buber wrote a book, *I and Thou*. His main point was there are two ways to relate to another person: as objects or as subjects. As objects, it means, "How can I use this person;" as a means to an end. As subjects, it means someone who comes to the encounter with needs and feelings of his or her own. You focus on the other person as a subject and give your full attention. It is no longer about doing favors in hopes that a favor will be returned, but about the relationship as a whole.

The primary person in Relationship Riches is you. It is your relationship with yourself, the longest relationship you will ever have. This does not mean that you only focus on yourself as your primary concern. Drop your self-consciousness about what you think is a flaw. When you are suffering (on the inside) people unconsciously pick up on your tension. You accept yourself and strive forward. This means that you work on yourself to remove fear, anxiety, worry, and self-centeredness. This results in becoming more joyful and warm-hearted. Your vitality and charm will begin to exude and people will be delighted to be around you. Shift your attention to other people. Why does this work? William James, an American philosopher, psychologist, and physician said, "The deepest drive in human nature is the desire to be appreciated."

Who, when they hear your name, "lights up" with a smile and is delighted to see and speak with you? Who in your life wants to be appreciated by you?

We often allow the greeting card companies to schedule our interactions because the advertisements, the store displays, and the internet banners are all screaming out to you. This can be helpful, but reaching out to a friend or family member, "just because," is often better. You don't need a reason. Like the Nike slogan, "Just do it."

Words of encouragement or appreciation can be shared if you know someone is working towards a goal. Checking in before the goal is completed can be just as reassuring as after the goal is met. If the situation is problematic and you show understanding and patience, your thoughtfulness will be well received. When you help to bring out the best in another person their self-esteem and confidence will grow.

Another important trait of being liked is to have a high tolerance in times of stress. You do not get irritated or annoyed easily. Those people with a high spiritual attitude often are more poised and even-tempered.

There is also a way to turn criticism into a positive situation. Apart from the lesson to be learned, you can expect criticism (ask any teacher or politician) and not be surprised by it.

The art of listening is one of the great secrets to being well-liked. Sometimes advice is not what is being sought-after, it is an open ear. Listen quietly, sympathetically, with love in your heart. This often helps the person to talk out their problems and find their own solutions. You will be liked for being a person who truly listens.

When you go a little deeper to find out what really is going on with someone who seems in a bad way, you can make more of a connection.

To gain a place in the heart of others, have an upbeat attitude, inspire others, and supply courage, strength, and appreciation. Lift someone's spirit.

The dialogue below with me, Sherrie Rose and *Scott Lovingood, Marxua Murphy,* Jeremy Stuzka, Ben Brooks, and Paulo Roldan, began when I shared a quote from Napoleon Hill in a Facebook group: *"One of the most important principles of success is developing the habit of going the extra mile."*

Scott responded: I honestly think the bar has been lowered in the last decade. Just going the extra few feet makes all the difference. So many people have decided to do just enough to get by. Doing above and beyond is seen as extraordinary these days.

Maruxa says: *I was just having lunch today with a successful marketer here in Austin, and we got on the topic of creating relationships that truly make an impact. The power of relationships that go above and beyond makes all the difference in the way marketing and selling works. I absolutely believe you can create more sustained money/income by growing relationships through being a valuable and extraordinary person. Sometimes, that extra-ordinary is the small things you do to show you care.*

Scott replied: *When I train our people every year I make sure they know this one key fact. If people like you, **they will forgive if you making a mistake**. You don't have to be perfect, you have to be liked. We are in the relationship business. We just happen to do our job while we build them. The relationship is what separates us from our competitors and where we can make the biggest difference in people's lives. We learn about our customers, feel for them and work to provide them the best value we can just like would for our friends and family. One lady in our office refers to every new customer as her New Best Friend.*

Jeremy replied: *Wow, that sounds exactly how my grandfather would describe business! ... The circle is closing!*

Ben says: *Treat every customer as the most important person in the world.*

Paulo says: *And the rest of your business partners should be treated the same way.*

Jeremy replied: *There was one progressive company I worked for. They taught me partners and co-workers are really internal clients, and thus should be treated as clients that you want to work with again. How you think about them makes all the difference to your happiness, which affects how you make that money and of course, the actual revenue generated.*

Relationships are powerful. From international relations to human social, interpersonal, intimate relations, relationships are the experience we have with each other here on planet earth.

You cannot separate relationships and conversations. How we collaborate and get along with each other is a factor on an international scale and a personal basis. Communication takes many forms.

Sometimes the best conversations have no words. Body language can speak volumes. A nod, a wink can be all the gesture you need to get your point across.

Conversations, whether online, text, or in person, are the basis of relationship building. Most commerce revolves around relationships whether business to business or business to consumer. Mathematical and database models also use the term relationship. Even automated businesses start with people planning the strategy and implementing the tactics. In business, and particularly if you are a coach or a consultant providing a service, you can use conversations to create trust and strong connections to build relationships.

Unfortunately, if you have bad habits in your personal relationships, then your conversation style spills over into business, and you may fall into patterns such as "talking over" each other, not listening or needing to 'being right' or wanting the last word. When this happens, the conversation then triggers fear, and judgment takes over. The neuroscience does not matter (but it is interesting to discover hardwired circuits in all human brain functions).

Daniel Goleman defines relationship management as the combination of your self-management and your social awareness to understand emotions in strengthening relationships with others.

Improving relationships begins with communication.

How you talk to your spouse, partner, children, and neighbors is the core of your conversation style.

Close relationships is one area of life where using positive psychology can make a big difference. According to Professor Shelly Gable, conversations are either active or passive and constructive or destructive. She found that out of four possible ways to respond to a partner's positive news, only the "active-constructive response" is good. Couples or business partners who react in any of three less positive ways are at greater risk of separating.

Consider the following example Gable gives to illustrate: Your significant other comes home, beaming, and announces that he/she just got a great promotion at work. You could react with:

1. Active-constructive response (BEST). "That's great, you've earned it, I'm so proud of you!" followed by questions. *Conveys enthusiasm, support, and interest.*

2. Passive-constructive response. "Great job, honey!" then shifting to the next topic. Like dinner.

3. Active-destructive response. "Wow! Does this mean you'll be working later hours? Are they going to be paying you more? I can't believe they picked you out of all the candidates." *Generally deflating.*

4. Passive-destructive response. Can take either of two forms: "Wow! Wait until I tell you what happened to me today," which is very self-focused, or, "What's for dinner?"—*Ignoring the event altogether.*

Moving into the business realm, because of the impact of financial gain and career advancement, when you improve conversations you tap the power of communication so you can create even deeper, more impressive results with your clients, team and the whole organization.

You don't need to be a business leader to take advantage of investing in Relationship Riches. However, it is true that you will find politicians, business and spiritual leaders at the core of those who are driving change and achieving superior results by leveraging communication and building relationships. Communication and cooperation have close ties.

In negotiation, the relationship often involves posturing and jockeying for position. If there is a transaction involved (Quid pro quo: you give me this, I'll give you that) that requires a contingency then, once the transaction is complete, the relationship may plateau and not grow.

In both our personal and business lives, if there is fear of conflict unless you are someone who does not mind confrontation and getting everything out on the table, then the ability to communicate with honesty and care, diminishes. Then there is a block and lack of movement and the relationship stagnates.

This is a good time to mention Stephen Covey's fifth habit – Seek first to understand, then to be understood. The rule is that understanding must precede any advice. The first goal of the conversation is only to understand, not to problem-solve. The reason that understanding must come first is because premature problem solving tends to shut people down and they close up. You want openness. Problem-solving and advice should only begin when both parties feel totally understood.

In business relationships, when there is a standstill, a mediator or communication coach is brought in to facilitate conversations. The goal is to help resolve conflict and deadlocks, and mediation is a voluntary process to settle disputes with an impartial third-party. What may also be uncovered are the interaction dynamics between the parties. If you are paying attention to the patterns (and breaking and interrupting the patterns), you may find that it strikes a chord and provides valuable insight. Then you can apply this going forward with your colleagues and other business relationships. Individuals, teams, and organizations can shift to conversations that fundamentally transform the future of the company. A positive side effect is that you can make decisions faster, with higher levels of wisdom and a greater ability to see the impact you have on others.

As we have evolved from the basic transaction, we move up to the transformational level where you'll find conversations that spark movements and organizations that want to change the world for the better. Core values are part of the transformation conversation and they encourage new ideas and openness.

Abraham Maslow's hierarchy of needs published in 1943, *"A Theory of Human Motivation,"* identified the highest motivation as self-actualization (defined as realizing personal potential, self-fulfillment, seeking personal growth and peak experiences). You must satisfy lower level basic needs before progressing on to be able to reach self-actualization and this is the transcending level where there is an awakening and giving component. There is a deep understanding that the culture and conversation within an organization impact not just profits and customer satisfaction, but how they are perceived as "doing good" in the world. The culture conversation is a mirror of the people and what they think about and how they act. The quality of relationship dialogue is what will take you and your organization to the transcendent level.

Who is making deals in business? Those who have built relationships. Who do you have on speed dial? That's Relationship Riches. And of course, those riches also mean more profits. Business relationships are likely the ultimate lever for making a difference in the world.

Relationship Riches in business give people the ability to have conversations that create businesses from the 'inside out' for more impact, more meaning, and more happiness for everyone involved.

Sherrie Rose lives by her motto: The Real Currency is Relationship Riches. When it comes to relationships, the foundation is LIKING in every relationship, both business and personal.

Sherrie has created several training programs and found one of the best ways to build relationships and have people get to know, like, and trust you is a webinar. She is a masterful webinar coach. She is an author, internet entrepreneur, and well-known in social media by her pencil-sketch profile illustration.

As a leading web event strategist, webinar coach, trainer and event host, Sherrie has guided students to success and has created and delivered numerous presentations, many of which are in perpetual "encore" mode using automation technology.

The Guru Series Interviews kicked off Sherrie's online business activity and she is fondly known for coining the term 'lovematism.'

Sherrie has two new books in the works: The Coach Revolution and Relationship Riches, based on her motto.

How I Accidentally Stumbled Into Making Millions Online Starting As A Kid

Bob Beckett

I was just 14 years old (some say I was 12), but I remember it like it was yesterday. I often joked, because I was all about sports, friends, and girls during the day, but at night I had a passion for where technology and the internet was heading. I learned how to program by the age of 11 and saw myself doing something to do with computers and the internet when I was older. I just didn't know what!

But this specific night was different. I was sitting in my parents' basement downstairs in their office, chatting with girls on good ole' AOL (behaving), as I remember seeing a banner popping up on the corner of my screen.

This banner said something along the lines of, "Make $100 Per Day Online Just By Sharing A Link!"

Now, obviously like most people, especially in the year 1996 when the internet was basically AOL, before Facebook and even Myspace was born...

The thought of making money on the internet wasn't a reality to most people yet. In fact, even to this day, most people don't see it as a reality! To take it even a step further, I still can't believe what I do and what many others do online is real, even 20+ years later! I wouldn't want to do anything else with my life as far as a career. If done right, you can create true time freedom!

Let's continue...

That one little banner changed my life forever. I took the link they gave me and spread it all over AOL and through different chat platforms and before you knew it, I was earning a good $4,000+ per month online as a kid!

Fast forward a few years later - Ebay came out when I was around 18 years old. I built a $3,000 to $8,000 profit per week business on that platform as a powerseller selling used Satellite equipment. I had three employees that would run around all the neighborhoods picking up all the out-of-contract equipment from "tiny classified ads" that I placed and two employees that would ship them out for me. Looking back, I don't know why I didn't scale it even further!

Fast forward another few years, I started to venture into Network Marketing. Now, I started off in the traditional Network Marketing arena, contacting my friends and family, doing hotel meetings across the country etc. I did pretty well, too!

Then I had my first daughter at the age of 20. I was at a week-long leadership meeting in San Diego and as I sat there looking at the ocean and all of God's creation I realized this isn't what I wanted. I wanted to create the freedom to stay home with my family and travel the world with those I love!

So when I came home, I decided to take my network marketing ventures online, and by the age of 21, I built an MLM organization doing over $750,000 per month in sales!

Oddly enough, I still had no idea how my success was happening other than I was hustling my face off every single day. It wasn't until I took a friend to Atlantic Beach while he was going through some hard times, that I realized where the real money was and why I was becoming successful over and over again.

A new company called ClickBank came out. If you don't know what ClickBank is, it's a marketplace of 10,000's of digital products for sale that you can sell as an affiliate and earn up to 75% commissions and even earn residual income!

While we were at the resort, I said, "Let's see if I can make some money from this digital product on ClickBank while we go out on the beach!"

I picked a digital product to sell, sent an email to my small 3,600 subscriber list and went and hung out on the beach for about 4 hours. Once I came back, we were both astonished! I generated over $1,800 in NEW residual income while I was getting rays and swimming in the ocean!

My friend said, "SEND AGAIN!" So of course, I did! And before our little 4-5 day trip was over, I generated over $4,000 in residual income from a tiny 3,600 email subscriber list!

This is when I realized, to make more money, I simply just needed a bigger list! So, for the next year straight I set out to learn how to build email subscriber lists 10x bigger and at a much faster pace. I built my list up to about 700,000 at that time, and the rest was history!

I would wake up in the morning, shoot out an email to my list that took me about 3 minutes to write, and would earn anywhere from $8,000 to $30,000 in a single day! Fast forward another 13 years, I'm still building massive lists, even into the millions, and helping other businesses do the same!

And when I look back to each one of my successful businesses in the past, even when I was 14, the reason I was successful was because I was building lists without even realizing it!

How You Can Build A Big List and Earn Huge Commissions Yourself!

Since you're reading this book it tells me a couple things about you right off the bat. You are inspired by others' success, and you are striving to succeed in your life as well! That says a lot about you!

With that said, you're most likely to have a passion in a certain niche. A niche that you feel you can truly help others in. One where you know for a fact that you can take someone from point A to point B and get them wherever they need to go faster!

This is called collapsing time, and people will pay you a lot of money for this! To the tune of $5,000 to even $20,000 or more! Think about it, how much traffic could you buy to build your list with just two $5k sales per month ($120,000 extra per year)?

Think people won't pay that much? I'll tell you for a fact that they do! We generate $100,000+ a month "extra" like clockwork without putting too much time into acquiring new customers!

You see, money is replaceable. Money replenishes every 1-2 weeks, but time you can never replace! Using what I'm about to share with you will hopefully allow you to create more time for yourself by generating a lot more money and hopefully working less (smarter), all while collapsing other people's time as well. A true win-win situation.

Don't think you can sell products or services for that high? Remember this, it takes the same amount of time and effort to sell a $7 to $97 product or service that it takes to sell a $5,000 to $20,000+ product or service!

Step 1: Find Your Passion

The first step is to find what you are truly passionate about! You'll know it's a real passion if it's something you can do for 12+ hours a day (if you wanted to) and it never feels like work!

Are you awesome at advertising? Can you drive the golf ball 250 yards dead straight every time? Maybe you are the "go to" person that everyone comes to when they need relationship advice? Whatever that passion is, there is usually a goldmine waiting for you on the other end!

Step 2: Figure Out Your Backend... FIRST!

Most of my coaching clients make the mistake of creating their front end products and services first when in reality, in my opinion, you should be developing backend coaching/services, or the end goal in mind first.

Now don't get me wrong, it's great to come up with a front end, but without your higher ticket products & services setup before you launch, or at least other people's in place as an affiliate, you will be missing out on what takes businesses from just a small mom and pop shop barely making it, to possibly making millions!

Let's say you wanted to create a new software that solves a certain problem for people. If you were to develop the backend first, you would know what the problems people are facing more in depth which will help you make your front end way more valuable.

Step 3: Find The ONE Thing That Sets You Apart and Give it Away

The third step is where my students usually get thrown off, but I promise you once you put this into practice a few times you'll get the hang of it quick! I am even going to give you access to a funnel template that you can just swipe from me to take out a lot of the "techy stuff" at the end of this chapter!

Here's all you have to do...

What is ONE secret, technique, or method that you can share with your target audience surrounding your passion that people would die to know?

Example: "Discover My #1 Technique For Driving 250+ Yards Every Time!"

"Discover My #1 Secret For Generating 50+ Leads Per Day!"

"Discover My #1 Advice For Healing A Failing Marriage!"

Once you have your ONE secret, technique, or method, we have to create a system around it that will generate you endless leads and sales, day in and day out.

First, create a quick video no longer than 30 to 60 seconds telling your website visitors the ONE promise that you will deliver on the next page after they give you their email address.

Second, and this is super important, create a video that's 5 to 8 minutes long that will go on the page right after they subscribed, that completely over-delivers on your promise to them! This is your ONE shot to blow their minds and gain their trust. It's also the one time that you will have 100% of your new subscriber's attention! You have to use this time to bridge them at the end of the video to your solution to their problems!

Step 4: Call to Action

Now, just like in the first video you created, you asked for the website visitor's email address. This is called a call-to-action. But merely just getting their email address won't pay the bills obviously. This is why at the end of your second video we have to to offer them your front end product or service, preferably at a trip-wire price to get more in the front door. This can be a $7 - $14.95 trial, where all we are trying to do is find out who is willing to pull out their credit card and who isn't. One of my mentors told me when I was around 20 years old, that the website that sort the fastest through people wins, and I couldn't have found that to be more true over the last 20 years!

Here is where the magic happens. This is my favorite part of the whole process because it equates to lots of money in the bank when done right! What I do after selling any products is either have a mid-ticket upsell product or get them to apply for a free strategy session!

Once they jump on a strategy session via video or phone, you once again blow their mind by figuring out their problems and solving them right there on the spot within 20-30 minutes. At the end of the video or phone conversation… simply ask if they want to work with you further! You would be shocked that when done right, a minimum out of 1 out of 4 will gladly hand you $5,000 to $10,000 for your services!

I put this whole process together in a step by step format, including the templates I promised earlier, and even the sales script that I have my assistants use before scheduling people into calls with me at http://live.highticketignition.com/sales-script !

As you can see, when done right, you can basically build an infinite email subscriber list while generating backend sales, and also have the ability to sell other people's products as an affiliate using this method. I hope that you got something out of this today, even if it just inspires you to just do a little more!

Thanks for Reading,

Bob Beckett

Bob Beckett is a family man first and is blessed to be a husband to his amazing wife and father of his four awesome kids! He "accidentally" started marketing online when he was just 14 years old by the Grace of God, and hasn't stopped since! He is a serial entrepreneur who has created several multi-million dollar businesses online over the years. Now, almost 34 at the time of this writing, he specializes in helping businesses develop their products and services, build sales funnels, and generate traffic and conversions! In other words, he helps businesses crush it online!

POWER OF PRAYER, POSITIVE BELIEF AND SUPPORT

SHERI ELSEN

The phone rang...it was 2:50am December 2, 2014. It was Ashley and she was in labor! I jumped out of bed, told my husband, Kenny, that Ashley was in labor, and I was headed to Kansas City. I stopped at the Kwik Shop, before my 4 hour drive, for a Pepsi and energy drink to help keep me awake. This was Ashley's second baby, another little girl! I was there two years ago for her first baby's birth as well. Parker Mae was born in January of 2013, so the girls were going to be about 22 months apart. Mark, Ashley's husband kept me up-to-date on Ashley's progress, and I knew I was going to be cutting it close, but I made it in time!

Kooper Jane was born December 2, 2014 and is grandchild #6. I stayed for a couple of weeks to help Ashley with the new baby. In the midst of all the excitement, I forgot about my yearly mammogram, that was scheduled for December 10th, 2014. I called and they rescheduled me for December 22th. I was thankful to get it done so quickly. I had an MRI in July and everything was fine - the spot that we'd been watching since May 2013 was unchanged.

The nurse practitioner came in the room and did a physical breast exam, then asked me if I had time for a sonogram, as they had seen a spot on my breast. I immediately asked if it was the same spot that we'd been watching on my right breast. She explained that it was a tiny spot on my left breast. She said that it was probably nothing, but since I was there, they would like to take look at it with the sonogram machine. Of course, I agreed.

After the specialist completed the sonogram, she said that the radiologist would read them and then be back in to talk to me. A few minutes later the radiologist and the nurse practitioner came into the room and said that the spot, although tiny, looked a little suspicious to them and suggested that I have a needle biopsy done. They explained that 80% of all lumps are benign.

They scheduled the biopsy for December 30th, 2014. Christmas was wonderful; I have a large family. My children, spouses, grandchildren, my mom, my sisters and their families...we totaled about 25. The only one missing was Aron, my son who lives in San Diego.

I let them all know about my biopsy, and asked them to say a prayer for me that day. The needle biopsy was not nearly as bad as I thought it was going to be! The nurse practitioner said that they should have the results the next day and wanted to know if I wanted to come back or just have her call me. I let her know good or bad, just give me a call. On New Year's Eve, 2014, I was working and received a call from the Breast Care Clinic, I left my desk and walked to a more private area so I could talk with the nurse. She told me that the tiny little spot was Cancer!

I had Breast Cancer! Even though I was not surprised, it was still extremely difficult to hear those words. My mind wandered as the nurse was explaining my options. I was more concerned with telling my family I had Breast Cancer. The nurse explained that due to the size of the lump, I had a couple of options, but I had already decided 10 years earlier what I would do if I was ever diagnosed with Breast Cancer. I asked her if it was my choice and she said of course it was, and I told her that I had decided 10 years ago that they both would both come off, a bilateral mastectomy. Unfortunately, this was not my first experience with cancer.

Ten and a half years earlier, in May of 2004, my twin sister, Shele, lost her battle with Breast Cancer! Shele was diagnosed with Stage IV Metastatic Breast Cancer at 38 years old. The prognosis for Metastatic Breast Cancer today is 33 months, but in 2004, it was even less. Shele was a fighter; she did every chemo and radiation treatment available. However, she lost her battle 10 months later. Watching Shele die was the hardest thing I've ever had to do in my life! I was with her in birth and in death, we had shared 39 birthdays together and so much more!

If you thought at the beginning of my story that Ashley was my daughter, you would be wrong, Ashley was Shele's only daughter. She was in college when her mother passed away, and calling her to let her know was the 2nd most difficult thing I've ever done. Before Shele died, I made a promise to her that I'd take care of Ashley and I'm now Grandma to her beautiful children. I wish Shele's cancer story was the only one our family experienced, but seven years after Shele's death, my mother was diagnosed with breast cancer.

My mom caught her Breast Cancer early and chose a bilateral mastectomy without reconstruction. Because she caught the cancer early and chose a bilateral mastectomy, her chemo was an oral pill that she had to take for five years. Now you understand why I wasn't surprised, but it was still devastating to know I, too, now had cancer! Telling my family was going to be hard as our experiences just have not been great! I've always been very strong and this experience with cancer was not going to be any different. I was sure I was going to beat this thing! I wasn't going to let this upset me or stop me from living my life!

I called my husband first and asked if he'd meet me. He's like me -strong! His response involved a few curse words, but then, "OK what's next? Let's get this taken care of!" Next was my daughter and she immediately started crying. I told her, "No tears!" I'm going to beat this thing! My response was pretty much the same when I broke the news to my sons, Ashley, mom, all of my sisters and close friends. Neither my sister nor my mom had chosen reconstruction, but I felt that reconstruction was the best option for me.

On February 19, 2015, I had both breasts removed with tissue expanders inserted to start reconstruction. To say the surgery was painful is an understatement, I've never been in so much pain! It felt like an elephant was sitting on my chest. The surgery went well, I was released the next afternoon. I had 4 drain tubes and was wrapped like a burrito! Recovery went well, I had some great support from my best friend and neighbor, June, as well as my daughter. They were in charge of changing my dressings and emptying the drainage bags! The year went by extremely fast and I did not have any issues with any stages of the process. Because I chose to remove both breasts, and the cancer was caught at an early stage, I only had to take an oral chemo pill. I have to take it for ten years.

There are definitely positive things that came out of breast cancer. 1. No more bra! (These girls don't go anywhere!) 2. I got to choose my breast size! I'm ½ the size I was before! 3. I joined a breast cancer support group, I'll tell you about these ladies later. Anyway, I finished my breast reconstruction right after Thanksgiving of 2015. We had a wonderful Christmas in 2016; I had added another grandbaby when Alex, and his wife welcomed a son, Mack Charles in October. I'm now up to seven beautiful grandbabies. 2016 was going to be a great year....so I thought! 2016 started wonderful when my daughter, Abby, added grandchild #8. Bentlee Marie was born in January of 2016.

In April of 2016 my mom was cleared at her 5 year check-up, which meant she was no longer required to take the oral chemo pill! In May 2016, Ashley added grandbaby #9, this time a baby boy, Meyer Lee, joined the world. July rolled around and I was needing a refill on my Thyroid medicine. I'd been diagnosed with hypothyroidism in November of 2011. I was seeing a new doctor for the first time, the doctor went over my history, all the usual stuff. One of his questions was, when was the last time I had a sonogram of my thyroid? I told him that I'd not ever had one. So he scheduled a baseline sonogram of my thyroid for the next week.

The scan found a couple of nodules on my thyroid, and they wanted to schedule a Nuclear medicine radioactive test. To do this I had to be off of my thyroid medicine for at least 6 weeks. The results of this test was inconclusive. The nodules were not cold or hot. Next, a needle biopsy! I had the needle biopsy done on Sept 19, 2016. Everything I read on thyroid nodules said that only a very small percentage of nodules were cancerous, so I wasn't too worried. I had just landed at the Madison airport for work when I received the call. The doctor was very apologetic for calling me and giving me the news over the phone, but she knew that I was traveling. It was cancer! I had cancer again! Papillary Carcinoma of the Thyroid! I had my thyroid removed on Halloween, 2016. An appropriate day to remove all that evil from my body, right? The recovery was nothing compared to the bilateral mastectomy!

They took my entire thyroid and several lymph nodes. There was involvement in my lymph nodes, and about half of them had cancer. The official diagnosis was Metastatic Papillary Thyroid Carcinoma. Treatment is Radioactive Iodine (RAI). Treatment couldn't be done for at least six weeks after my thyroid surgery, so that put it close to Christmas. With nine grandchildren, I didn't want to miss out on Christmas, so I scheduled my treatment for January 13, 2017. Thyroid cancer is one of the most curable known cancers. I'm very blessed that both of my cancer diagnoses were mild. Cancer is never easy to hear, let alone hear twice. I look forward to 2017 and being cancer free again!

When I had the opportunity to tell my story in Everyday Hero's II, I really wasn't sure what message I could deliver, but after taking time to write my story down, I think I have a clear message, especially for those just diagnosed or still fighting cancer.

Get support! Don't go it alone!

I'm a strong, stubborn, self-sufficient person, and really thought I could do this with just the support of my immediate family and friends. I was wrong. I joined a support group about halfway through my reconstruction. The Breast Friends group has shown me what it means to belong to a group where everyone understands what you are going through! They have taken me in and given me a purpose! We want to continue this support to all of you that are fighting Breast Cancer and all of you who are survivors by providing online support. To find out more, visit www.ForeverBreastFriends.com Please join us supporting each other through our fight and survivorship of this ugly disease. We'd love to help you as you travel through this life journey, for ALL of YOU are Everyday Heroes!

Sheri Elsen has a passion for life!

She is a compassionate, kind, considerate, caring everyday wife, mother, grandmother, sister, daughter to a very special family.

Sheri lives in a small Kansas town, which she was born and raised in as well as has raised her own children. She is a two-time cancer survivor who cares deeply about supporting and encouraging all cancer survivors with a special desire to help those with breast cancer.

Sheri has been blessed to be part of an outstanding support group and is extending that support online with ForeverBreastFriends.com. Sheri considers herself blessed to have lead a great life and is looking forward to dedicating the next chapter in her life to being an entrepreneur and life coach.

CREATE AN AMAZING LIFE THROUGH WORK-LIFE BALANCE

ZANE CORRIHER

By a split second I missed a big accomplishment. About half an hour earlier my seven-year old daughter and I walked hand in hand into her gymnastics class. Her little face was glowing with pure joy because I was finally able to tear myself away from work and be there.

So there I sat, hunched in the plastic, blue chair as my daughter tumbled and flipped on the other side of the room. And it was on this particular day that she finally navigated the balance beam by herself and dismounted gracefully. Perfection!

Only, I had missed it. My face was buried in my phone, handling an *important* email. And I missed her moment of triumph. And she knew it. The look of hurt on my daughter's face still haunts me.

It was the same look of hurt that I would see on my wife's face when I was late to dinner. Not the first time though, because she understands that things happen. Not the second, third or tenth time either. But eventually, she came to expect that I'd be late because I *had* to take that phone call. Because I *had* to answer a few more emails. Because I *couldn't* leave the meeting on time – someone needed me for something important. Yet, today, I can't remember what that important thing was or what the email was about or who I needed to call.

I do remember her face though. Because my wife is important. My daughter is too. But so is work.

I was moving up incredibly fast at a Fortune 100 company, spending less than 2 years at any given job before winning another promotion. I coach, train, and oversee the personal and professional development of employees in North, Central, and South

America as well as parts of Western Europe. It's an awesome job and I love what I get to do every day (I know, I'm lucky, but it wasn't always that way).

I was also building a business where I helped people rewire their brains to become peak performers through an audio technology I'd developed. Sitting behind my desk until 2AM, seven days a week for 80 hours had become normal. And I loved it.

But there was my family, and they missed me. And the look on their faces every time I got buried under my work ripped my heart out. Every. Single. Time. Because I missed them too.

So to balance things, I began cutting back on work – and I got behind. I started spending more time with my wife and daughter – by which I mean my body was present. But my face was often in my phone. My brain was consumed with projects and clients. So, I started skipping sleep, grabbing maybe 3-4 hours a night. I felt thin, sort of stretched, like butter scraped over too much bread (to quote Bilbo Baggins from Tolkien's Lord of the Rings).

I was completely out of balance. And quite frankly, I wasn't sure how to change it. I was overworked, stressed out, and fighting to hang on to happiness.

The greater tragedy though is how utterly ordinary this problem is. Because nearly every corporate professional I talked to struggled with balance. Nearly all of them wished they owned their own business so they could control their time and workload. And so I started speaking with full-time entrepreneurs to find out how they managed their days and I discovered that they struggled with the same thing! Clearly, the one thing that unites most successful people is the elusive search for work-life balance.

But it wasn't always that way. Because when I was a kid, things seemed easier. The school part wasn't my favorite thing (other than recess which was awesome), but the freedom to climb trees, rip the knees out of my jeans, ride bikes and play basketball 'til the sun disappeared was pretty epic. I never had to think about balance back then because it was kind of baked into my life: Get up, go to school, do homework, play until my legs buckled from glorious exhaustion, go to bed and repeat.

Life was good. But then college happened. And there were term papers, reading lists, socializing, and parties, and more socializing…

The scales of balance began to tilt. I felt like I had to choose between working hard and enjoying my personal life. For the next four years the scales tipped to my social life.

College was fun. Grad school was different. I began staying up later reading book after book, writing paper after paper. I did my best to cram in a social life, but failed miserably in most cases. The scales tipped the other way.

And then I went to work. As a single guy, I could pour myself into my career. There were moments I wished I had more time to spend with friends – but I was focused on climbing the ladder. Balance wasn't a big consideration.

But then a girl stole my heart. And then a few years later she gave birth to a baby for whom I swore I would do *anything*. And then that baby turned seven years old. She was same little girl who wore a light blue leotard, standing there looking across the gymnastics floor at me, hurt and disappointed, because I couldn't keep my face out of my phone for an hour.

What happened?

If this story sounds familiar, then I assure you that you're in good company. Because the Disneyesque videos and images people decide to show you on social media are typically masking a difficult reality: Most people struggle to balance their life.

That's because our brains are set up to be able to process a pretty simple life. Humans are really good at figuring out how to find food, make love, have babies, raise them in small communities and survive predators, extreme weather, and hostile tribes.

But then we progressed rapidly from agrarian societies to industrialization and then on to the information age. Our cultures, economies and technologies have evolved faster than the human brain has been able to adapt. So despite modern conveniences, people stumble around feeling lost, overwhelmed, and unfulfilled.

To compensate, we do our best to cobble together work habits in the midst of figuring out exactly *how* to do our jobs and run our businesses. And then we strive to figure out how to be a spouse, parent and friend as we create our lives.

It's a lot like putting together a complex Lego set without instructions or a complete picture of what you're building – you'll end up in a frustrating cycle of breaking things down and starting over again. Or maybe you'll decide to accept a barely functional representation of what you were working to build. Or you'll simply throw your hands up and declare that the thing you're trying to create isn't possible.

This won't lead to balance.

Neither does the approach to balance most people take which is to divide their lives into thirds: Eight hours of work, eight hours of personal time, and eight hours of sleep.

I know people who have achieved a life of perfect thirds. And they are miserable. I also know people who work 80 hours a week and spend quality time with their families. And they love their lives.

Balance has very little to do with time. In fact, if there was some magical guru out there who could grant you 10 days a week, I can guarantee that you'd fill your extra 3 days with stress, unnecessary work and inefficiency. Your personal time would also feel lackluster and unfocused as well.

That's because balance isn't primarily about time. It's about developing external disciplines that will make up for the limitations of your evolving, adapting mind. Balance is created when you train your brain to cope with a world that is set up to cram as much stress, overstimulation, and unrealistic expectations as it can into your skull.

Balance is created by slowing life down so that you can wrench your face away from your phone and be completely present with your kid for an hour as she does something for the first time – and watching her revel in the joy of simply knowing that you saw it.

I craved balance. And so I read about it. I studied people who had it.

I learned how to put myself in successful positions by leveraging my strengths. At the same time, I figured out how to reduce the times I found myself in situations where I was naturally limited or unskilled.

I learned how to prioritize, eliminate hidden time wasters, and make every minute count.

I mastered my craft (and continue to do so), because mastery creates speed of work and decision velocity.

I discovered how to let go of my limits and self-defeating stories that had been holding me back for most of my life.

I learned how to network effectively and authentically while creating quality relationships along the way.

I became present at home so that I could focus on the people I love in the time we spend together.

I learned how to fill my life with people and activities I enjoy after creating the productivity habits to make that happen.

I love every aspect of my life. It isn't perfect, but it's amazing.

And so I started another business devoted to teaching people how to create work-life balance. I've helped countless people achieve this level of balance and it's been life changing for all of them, resulting in more success and fulfillment in their professional and family lives.

People who achieved balance started making more money, got promoted faster, and grew their businesses. The hidden gem is that when you create balance, you become more successful in every aspect of your life.

With some work and focus, this level of balance can be achieved by anyone. And I'm here to tell you that it's possible for you.

You aren't always going to love every moment. There are going to be dirty diapers in there somewhere. But perhaps the greatest thing balance does is create unfathomable happiness in those who achieve it. I believe that's what most people are after if we're being honest with ourselves.

Zane Corriher is a work-life balance and peak performance expert. He helps successful professionals develop mindsets and habits that create an elite life. To learn more or to work with him directly, you can contact him at: www.DevelopingLifeBalance.com, by email at zanecorriher@gmail.com; or call him directly at (919) 597-8518.

Your Blueprint To Success

Richard Krawczyk

It was the summer when I was about 12 years old that I experienced something life-shifting. When you live in a small town such as Lake In The Hills, IL with a population of 5,000 (1983) and something new happens, all the neighbor kids take notice, since nothing much ever changes.

One day, I saw a couple of men drive up in a truck to a vacant lot. A car pulled up behind them. The men had some large rolls of paper and the woman in the car had some apparatus she set up and looked through. Like any kid, I was curious to find out what they were doing. The lot had been vacant for a long time. It was a blank slate, yet nothing ever manifested there.

A trailer was set up on the site. More people came. Pickup trucks, dump trucks, and machines with large shovels to dig. There were groups of people that would meet each morning to look at the large rolls of paper. They seemed to be discussing something, and then they would all head out and start doing something on the land.

Just before dusk, the group would meet again to review the drawings. They talked back and forth, and by the shake of their heads, they had agreed on some things. Each day they reappeared to do it all over again. This process of meeting, looking at the large rolls of paper, and doing things took about a month.

There was progress each day. Where there was not an indentation in the ground, there was now a hole dug for a basement. Where there was no foundation for a building to be constructed, a foundation had been laid. Where there was not a wall, there was now 2 x 4 framing. Each day there was progress. Some days it rained and less was done, but the team always met and looked at the drawings.

My curiosity got the best of me. I walked to the site and asked to speak to the person in charge. "What are those rolls of paper that everyone looks at every day?"

The foreman said, "They are blueprints. A blueprint is a guide that shows all of us exactly what we need to do to create the house that our clients have hired us to build for them. Without it, we would be lost. If we do not follow the blueprint exactly, the heating system might not work, the doors may not close, and if the foundation is not right the whole thing could come crashing down around us. That's how important the blueprint is."

As you can tell from this story, I was witnessing the building of a home.

As I watched this process, several things intrigued me. First, there was the group of people that met each day. Second, there was an air of cooperation and action. Most important, there were the rolls of paper - the blueprint. The success of the project seemed to be in the blueprint and following it exactly as written.

Every day the group or team of people met, looked at the blueprint, and then went into action.

There is a Blueprint for Everything

So what does building a house have to do with you? Everything.

Wouldn't it make sense that, if there were blueprints to build a house, a car, and a successful, loving relationship, that there would also be a blueprint to be successful in life?

The difference between successful people and people who want to be successful is as simple as following a blueprint. The point is that when you build anything - say for instance a house, car, business, fulfilling relationship, political campaign, movie or healthy body - you need a blueprint. Not just a desire or a dream, but you need the actual blueprint in order to implement the plan.

Just as you would build a house, your dream or desire must follow the blueprint or the very foundation itself will be flawed. A flawed foundation only means that everything you thought you might be able to realize, in fact, your whole life, may come crashing down around you. Too many times, people want to build their skyscraper of life on a foundation of a house and wonder why they consistently fail. The more solid your foundation, the greater level of success you will experience

When you choose to do or not do certain things, you will produce specific results. This blueprint works all the time for everybody.

It was about 10:00 pm on a typical Chicago December winter night. There was an eerie stillness in the crisp, cold air. The twelve inches of snow on the ground was not enough. An additional three inches was expected to fall that night. The bone-chilling wind from nearby Lake Michigan made spending the night on a park bench, near the Northwestern University campus, not an option. The twenty-three degrees felt even colder through his summer jacket—the only jacket he owned. By morning, he would surely be dead.

"If I want to make it through the night alive, I need to find shelter," he said to himself.

Luckily, the nearby Burger King was open 24 hours a day—one of the *benefits* of being homeless near a university. Even at 25, his baby face made him look much younger. With his baseball cap and backpack, he could have easily passed for a typical college student.

The young man looked forward to warming up his near-frozen fingers as he ordered a cup of coffee, which came with unlimited refills. When he sat down and looked around, everyone was reading or studying something. To blend in and not bring attention to himself, he opened up his backpack. He took out a book on personal development and began to read.

This young man's journey began that first cold night.

He repeatedly read the book. The strategies started to seep, one by one, into his sorry, broken soul.

How did he wind up in this dire situation?

He had made money in the past, yet, had foolishly spent it before he made it. Thinking his big ship had come into the harbor—meaning that he was about to be wildly successful—he failed to save any money.

Working with an investment banking firm in downtown Chicago, he put together a deal worth $25 million to him. However, as quickly as the winds on Lake Michigan can whip up, the deal was blown away, and his whole world came crashing down around him.

An unscrupulous individual with a big ego messed up the deal, leaving him no part of that $25 million in potential profits.

It would have been good money for a kid, yet he ended up empty handed.

He had only a few real friends. One of them would sneak from his parent's house to give this newly homeless person some leftovers from dinner—which was the only food he had each day. He had too much pride to ask for help and refused to let his family know about his downward spiral.

He continued to expand his newfound knowledge during this unscheduled break in his life. Getting a few hours of sleep after reading books at the local library during the day, he continued to read at night at the Burger King—where no sleeping was allowed.

At one point, while looking up at the sky one day, he chuckled to himself. Half-jokingly, he said to God, "OK. Enough of this! Can you please hurry up this dark part of my life so I can become the person I'm destined to become?"

_____

You may be shocked to learn that the baby-faced, homeless person was me over twenty-five years ago.

Today, I am a highly sought-after motivational keynote speaker, best-selling author, and a human potential expert.

My intention of telling you this story was not to impress you but to impress upon you that anyone can become successful—even a homeless person with a goal.

How did I go from being homeless to giving talks in front of thousands of raving fans with my empowering message of success?

If your starting point is better than homeless, you are already way ahead in the game of life - or at least ahead of where I started.

But... (Isn't there always a "but?")

You will have to trust this process and start with a clean slate.

Let's face it…

If your life were already perfect, you would not be reading these words. At this point in your life, there is obviously something that is not working for you. So let's work together to fix it.

It's time to learn what is holding you back and learn how to instantly blast through your obstacles.

Richard Krawczyk

Known as "Mr. Blueprint," Richard Krawczyk is a best-selling author, public speaker, marketing consultant, social media influencer, investor, and business strategist. His credentials include a lifetime of entrepreneurial success. He is a leading authority in the areas of achievement, motivation, and peak performance.

When Richard is not on the road speaking, he leads several multi-day events, executive coaching programs, and his exclusive mastermind group, in addition to his thriving corporate consulting practice.

Website: http://TheMrBlueprint.com

Twitter & Instagram: @TheMrBlueprint

BLAZE YOUR OWN TRAIL

REED FLOREN

From a young age, I discovered that I wanted to blaze a trail of my own and have the freedom and flexibility to enjoy life on my terms.

On the first day of Kindergarten, my dad lost his job. It took my dad over a year to find a comparable job. We ended up living off credit cards and shopping at thrift shops/garage sales. From this hardship, I learned that there is no such thing as job security. My dad found a job that was 150 miles away round-trip. He commuted to work 3 hours every day. Because of how much time my dad spent working/driving I didn't get to see him much and I knew that I wanted it to be different for my children.

In elementary school, I started acting in plays and by middle school I was acting at the local college. This gave me confidence to speak in front of large audiences.

On March 29, 1998, a tornado destroyed many houses in my town. We were without electricity for weeks. My dad ended up canceling TV service, which is still not reactivated. I credit the hardship of the tornado and the time spent not watching television with allowing me to focus on learning.

Then came 7th grade...I went to new student orientation and quickly realized that the local middle/high school was not for me. All they could tell us was what we couldn't do. I hated it. We started looking for alternatives, and my dad's former colleagues introduced us to this unique school called the Minnesota New Country School (MNCS) http://www.newcountryschool.com

What made the school unique was you would work on projects that interested you instead of being told what to do. Your learning was at your own pace and at your own level.

With a computer on my desk all day long, I began spending a lot of time on the Internet. I started searching for ways to make money.

I stumbled on a program called AllAdvantage.com which paid $0.50 an hour to surf the Internet; all you needed was to install their software which displayed a banner advertisement at the bottom of your screen. You also would get paid $0.10 an hour for every hour people that you recruited were online.

I ended up signing up my parents and a bunch of college kids. This was my first lesson in the power of leverage. I could make money off other people doing work.

Since MNCS is a small school and we didn't have a cafeteria of our own, one of the local restaurants would cater a lunch to us every single day. These lunches would go for $1.75 and you had a choice from about 20 different meals a day to choose from. I would sell various parts of my meal to the students. I don't like pickles, and my cheeseburger would come with three. I would sell each pickle slice for $0.50 a piece and nearly pay for my entire lunch!

I would also buy six packs of Mountain Dew and sell them for $1 or a lunch ticket ($1.75) per bottle. Some days I would bring candy into school and I would sell them for about a 10X markup. I would always have $20 or more in $1's in my wallet I would make small loans of $1 or so to my friends when we were on field trips and charge interest that doubled the next day.

During my 8th grade year at MNCS, my school was awarded a multi-million-dollar grant from the Bill and Melinda Gates Foundation to replicate the school all over the country. They hired me as an independent contractor to help, while I was in school on certain projects of theirs for at least $10 an hour and oftentimes on a project basis of $1,000 or more.

I ended up helping them put on workshops where I spoke all over Minnesota about education, created information products to market the school, and I worked with a National Geographic videographer to make some very professional looking videos to teach others about MNCS.

I started doing other technical and video work as an independent contractor for other local businesses. I even hosted training after school and charged people for computer instruction.

In 2003 there was a fantasy stock market simulation game which allowed us to buy and sell real stocks with a simulated $100,000 of cash. I was number one and had made $140,000 within a few weeks. I ended up getting greedy and made riskier investments which dropped me down to $77,000. I went from the #1 spot to the bottom. Within 90 days of hitting rock bottom of went from $77K to a whopping $2.3 million dollars in my account. I won the game.

With this dramatic success in the stock market I ended up buying every stock market book and training program I could get my hands on and opened a brokerage account so I could trade stocks while I was at school. I decided to teach others how to research stocks and make money with the stock market. I ended up joining various forums and discussion boards on investing and I posted advice on the stock market. I even started hosting a local meetup group for stock market investors.

In a short time, I had developed a loyal fan base, which was asking me to create my own site, so they could spend their time focused on my systems and learning from me.

To achieve success, you need to develop a loyal base of customers and give them what they want; success is easy then.

I got a cease and desist letter from a large financial newspaper for having a website name too similar to their established brand. Now as a teenager, I had no idea about copyrights or trademarks and I was devastated that a business I highly admired wasn't happy with me. It didn't take long for other publications to get wind of the story; I was getting my 15 minutes of fame.

In 2004 and 2005, my senior year of high school, I realized that I could achieve real success from the Internet. My stock market site was ranked number one on Google, Yahoo and MSN (Bing).

I ended up trying lots of strategies to make money online and did a senior presentation to a hungry group of over 100 adults on how to make money on the Internet.

Shortly after graduating from high school I ended up investing in a course which taught me how to become a joint venture (JV) broker. A JV broker lines up people who have a product to sell with affiliates/JV partners who can promote it and then take a percentage of the sales. I ended up buying the JV course from Russell Brunson's affiliate link and his bonus was that you could broker one of his products in return for investing in the course.

I eventually connected with Mark Joyner who gave me a ticket to my first Internet marketing conference and I met hundreds of marketers and this gave me the opportunity to work one on one with a marketer named Henry Gold.

In December of 2005, Henry and I teamed up and we launched a web site called 117ChristmasGifts.com which is a massive list building giveaway. We got over 1,000 joint venture partners to participate and at the end of the month had built a list of over 50,000 new members!

In March of 2006 I had literally cracked the AdSense code and was spending money on Google AdWords to send traffic to my sites which had articles and AdSense advertising on them. By April 2006 I was on track to make $30,000 per month before Google decided to shut me down.

This was a devastating loss for me as I was living relatively high on the hog for a young kid. I had bought a bunch of new expensive toys including my first car.

It took me several months to recover from that loss and I decided the best way for me to make money was to build my own list. I did a JV giveaway event and I invited only 10 marketers to participate; we built a list of over 3,000 people in just 7 days.

Within one week of building my list I was one of the top affiliates for a product. I ended up making over $1,000 in commissions and winning a Skype Cordless Phone from my affiliate efforts. This began a long stream of placing in or winning affiliate competitions.

I brokered hundreds of products for various marketers and spoke at different events. I even started hosting my own events with Jeff Mills every month in the Minneapolis metro.

In 2007 I sold over 100 copies of my own coaching program on joint ventures. I learned that you could get paid upfront before creating a course by offering it as live group coaching.

In 2008 I became a dad; my son Zachary was born. Becoming a parent has had a tremendous impact on my life and my business as it FORCED me to focus on my priorities.

In 2009 I started doing a lot of high ticket coaching and consulting between $1k-$5K. I would work with a lot of new marketers and help them build their first email list. I got invited to speak in London and eventually started having my own events there too. I started camping fulltime in my own motorhome because I had gotten the travel bug and I wanted to prove that you could make money online from anywhere even in a remote location like a campground.

In 2010 I spoke all over the US, Canada, England, Australia, New Zealand, Singapore, Malaysia and Hong Kong. I also developed a successful site called SoloAdDirectory.com where I show the results I have from solo ads that I have purchased.

In 2011 my son Connor was born in London. I had met his mother while speaking in England. We eventually filed for her to immigrate to the United States so we could get married.

In 2012 after only 6 months of marriage I filed for divorce which led to a nasty custody battle. I had a team of four attorneys working around the clock at hundreds of dollars an hour each and it just sucked my energy and savings and I spiraled into depression.

My divorce was finalized late 2013 and my ex-wife and son moved back to England. During my divorce, I had a very hard time focusing on business and essentially, it fell apart.

In 2014 I released a bunch of new training products on the WarriorForum/WarriorPlus I ended up having 10 courses in a row get product of the day. I replenished my savings and even started investing in the stock market again.

I also placed in a ton of affiliate contests and used a lot of paid traffic strategies to market other people's products in addition to using my list. I credit much of my success in 2014 to my girlfriend who motivated me to get out of my funk.

In 2015 and 2016 I focused more on affiliate marketing and only put out a handful of my own products or products with partners.

It's now 2017 and I want to take what I've learned in my lifetime and help a lot of entrepreneurs achieve the success they are looking for.

If you want to be a successful entrepreneur you need to never give up on your dream, focus on learning new strategies and always provide massive value. There will be hardships but if you do the right thing you can overcome anything!

Reed Floren has been marketing online since 1999 and has had many ups and downs in his career.
From his story, you will learn why you should never give up on your dream, why you need to focus on learning new things and why providing massive value is the only way to achieve true success. To learn more about Reed visit
http://www.reedfloren.com

THE BEST CHRISTMAS EVER

LAURA HORAN

Society always says it's the people with the biggest smiles on their faces are the ones who have had the toughest lives. This is not because they are trying to hide what is going on or ashamed of what is happening in their life, it's because they train themselves to see the world differently.

Problems only become problems if you let them. From a young age I learnt my problems would make my life a daily struggle unless I challenged them. For every negative situation in my life I'd do what I could to get rid of it. If I couldn't do that, then I would have to change my mindset or do something active to control how much of my life would be consumed by this issue.

There are three struggles I have faced in my life that have affected my mental health, one of them no longer affects me. The struggle of being homeless from the age of 8 until I was 12 is now something I can discuss without feeling sad, anxious or scared. This is because I actively did something about it.

My dad left me when I was only a couple of months old and at the age of 2 my Mam found someone who made her happy. From the outside everything was perfect. The three of us lived in a beautiful home, went on trips and were friends with all the neighbours.

My Mam suffered with bipolar disease nearly all her life and struggled to live a normal life. Bouncing back and forth to doctors to adjust medication, she now describes periods of our lives together 'a bit of a blur'.

My Mam was always a hard worker, enjoying socializing with people and keeping active. She worked in a sewing factory and then in retail up until we became homeless. My Mam's boyfriend who I nicknamed 'The Grinch' as a child always wanted everything perfect. He could never understand I was only a child and children make mistakes. He terrified me and for a while he would just shout and threaten me.

Sometimes when I think back I wonder if I imagined it. I was so young - how could he hit me? The fear of him hurtingr5 me was always worse. I would shake and jump and cry hoping he wouldn't get angry when I'd make a mess or forgot to do something.

At the age of eight, I couldn't lie to my Mam anymore. I had to tell her because I was getting older and it was getting worse. It felt like forever when I was planning to tell her because I didn't know if she would get mad or what he would do.

The day I told her, I have never seen my Mam so angry. I was terrified. When he came home from work my Mam jumped on him hitting him and screaming. I ended up ringing the police after the window of the front door was smashed.

My Mam struggled badly with her mental health after the breakup. We ended up with no money and nowhere to live.

Although my Mam wasn't well, she always made every day fun. We would bounce from family's homes to friends' homes, from floor to floor without me realising the situation we were in. I didn't walk around sulking, because I was hanging out with my Mam who was my best friend, every day going on crazy adventures! She had such an amazing imagination and could turn O'Connell Street into New York City or make a game out of cars going by. We didn't need anything - we had each other.

Up until I was ten, we did this and had overstayed our welcome in other people's homes. Also my Mam's pride had been taking a beating for too long. I believe it's a horrible situation to be in but my Mam and I would never expect to be able to sleep on people's floors or couches forever. Your home is supposed to be comfortable and coming home to people you're not used to hanging around your house is not comfortable for anyone and the majority of people that did help us out didn't have spare rooms there. They were just scraping by themselves.

My Mam and I moved into a homeless shelter near town. It was at the end of a road in a normal looking housing estate. It had a large drive in and high walls so the building was not clearly visible from the outside. When you walked up to the door it just looked like a typical old bed and breakfast. There were dirty tiles on the floor when you walked in and electrical wires coming out of the walls. There were approximately fifteen to twenty families living there.

How the workers treated the residents so differently still annoys me. My Mam was not the stereotypical homeless woman. She wasn't on drugs, she wasn't an alcoholic and she made herself presentable every day. Because of that, we were given a huge bedroom with two bunk beds, one with a double bed on the bottom and another single bed. There was enough room for 5 to 6 people to sleep here. Meanwhile, a woman we made friends with was sharing a double bed with her husband and two children.

For several months I stayed in my bubble of happiness and embraced all the great things in my life. I was smart in school and so enjoyed learning, I spent lots of time with my family and I was back in my old school with my friends. A vivid memory that really helped me keep positive was spending time with my hamster, Sarah. Pets were strictly not allowed in the shelter but I was begging my Mam for one. She eventually gave in and I spent every day sneaking my hamster in carrier bags to bring to the park or library. She went everywhere with me! One time she got out of her cage and she was lost for a couple of days. My Mam was so panicked they would find her and we would get in trouble. We found her buried behind the sink after making a nest for herself.

This bubble was then popped just before Christmas that year. I had been in school learning about the homeless. At the time I didn't see myself as homeless and the word was never said around me. So my Mam didn't see an issue with me talking learning about the homeless people because I was oblivious to the fact that I was one of them. In school we had to put together a shoebox with old toys to give to homeless children for Christmas. I was so excited to help. I went to my Nana's house and got toys from the attic and wrapped them nicely inside a shoebox. A few weeks later Santa was coming into the shelter to give out presents. There was a big tree in the reception, all the children were going crazy decorating the tree, making cards and telling Santa what they wanted for Christmas. He opened the big black sack of toys and begun giving them out. Before I was even handed one I looked around and noticed the boxes they were opening were shoeboxes. It was like time stood still and everything just dawned on me all at once. I was so annoyed at my teachers for how they described the homeless children and how they looked in pictures. Being portrayed as dirty and uneducated. This idea of how the world saw the homeless was not how I viewed myself.

After this happened, the first thing I did was run to my friend, Rosie, in the shelter. She was a couple of years older than me, but all the other children were too young for me to play with. I told her about what just happened and asked her question after question about our situation. She quickly left me loss for words when she answered that she's been living in shelters for six years. To me this was a prison sentence. I was disgusted that people were left in these emergency accommodations for so long.

I became a lot more bitter during the rest of my time in the shelter and for my teenage years. I would get so annoyed looking at the men running the shelter watching TV in their office, playing on their computer and laying on their comfy couches with not a care in the world while there were children crying and begging for food off people in the shared kitchen.

Luckily before the following Christmas, my Mam and I were housed. The first thing I asked when shown around the apartment was 'How long has this apartment been here' and they said four years. The apartment had been empty before us. I didn't understand why we were homeless for so long if this apartment was here and I thought all our suffering was for nothing.

That Christmas my Mam and I had a blow-up bed, portable dvd player, dvd's and a 30-inch Christmas tree. Not even a fridge in the house and it was the best Christmas of my life because we had finally made it.

When I reached final year in school, I realized I could continue this destructive path I was on as a teenager or I could prove everyone wrong and make something of myself. I spent that whole year, day and night, studying for the points I wanted. I wasn't the bright child in class, I was the one who was always in detention and getting into mischief. I knew if I wanted to do well I'd have to work harder than anyone. But I did it - I got one of the highest results in my year, I got into DCU and now I am nearly finished final year doing a Journalism Degree. I have had and continue to get great experience in different jobs relating to my career. I am the Deputy Events Manager for the Media Production Society and Deputy Images Editor for The College View. I strive on pushing to do more, and every year I have gone above and beyond my goals. At the age of twenty, I am so proud of what I have achieved and I believe no matter what your background is you can do anything once you have the right mindset.

In 2016 I got a chance to actively do something about the pain this experience has brought me. Along with the Media Production Society in Dublin City University we raised €15,000 euro for The Peter McVerry Trust (a charity which helps homeless people) during their 24-hour broadcast event. I got the opportunity to tell my story and give back to the homeless community. I also raised much needed awareness on the situation by getting many publications online, in print and on radio to tell my story. I also got to go onto The Ray D'Arcy TV show to further push the issue.

Leaving DCU is going to be so difficult for me as I am surrounded by people I love and I will miss the atmosphere of this big community who run and attend events together weekly to educate each other more. Still, I am so excited to grow my career around media and telling stories.

Thank you for reading my story.

Laura Horan is a twenty-year-old finishing her last year in DCU. After a difficult childhood, Laura was tackling depression and going towards a life filled with drink and drugs. She motivated herself to study hard and managed to get one of the highest results in her year.

Over the last three years, she has been very successful in her journalism career having publications with The Independent, Oxygen.ie, The Irish Sun, Campus.ie and The Irish Times. Laura has also had the opportunity to discuss social issues on TV shows like The Ray D'Arcy show and radio stations such as FM104, Newstalk and Beat102. Recently Laura has been working on a documentary on European Poverty, which will be aired on ARTE TV soon.

During her years in college she embraced the community involvement and became Deputy Events Officer for the award winning Media Production Society and Deputy Images Editor for The College View Paper.

NEVER GIVE UP

KELLY COLE

Hey you - yeah you! It's very important that you never ever give up! Make up your mind what you want and Go For It with everything you have inside you! I remember playing football my freshman year in Chicago at Weber High school, which, by the way, was the same high school as Mike Krzyzewski aka Coach K, head coach of the Duke Blue-Devils. At the start of the season we were so excited and had high hopes of having a great season. When we came out and lost our first three games, I was so upset and told the coach I was quitting! I remember the exact play when I made up my mind I was quitting. Our cornerback had just got burnt down the sideline on a 60 yard bomb pass, as I'm watching the guy run down the sideline heading toward the end-zone, I just walked off the field. I could not go through a whole season of not winning one game, like I did all my previous years of playing pee wee & midget football, I told the coach "I'm done!"

My coach told me, "Cole do not quit this team!"

I said "Coach I'm Done!, I Quit""

He said "Cole do not quit, if we win all of the rest of our games we have a great chance to be the district champions and all I'm asking you to do is not give up on me and the team."

I said "OK I won't quit, but we better turn this thing around ASAP or I'm out!"

After the game, Coach told us all to take a seat and pay attention to the chalkboard. He wrote down a list of our last seven games, which happened to be the toughest teams in the district! He told us all he wanted us to do is take it one game at a time and commit to giving every play the utmost respect. He said "I want you to promise to REP!" "I want you to Respect Every Play and Never Give Up!" He said "Can you all make that promise to me?" Everyone agreed. The next day at practice my coach walks up to me and hands me a bag. I said "What's this?" He said "Just open it, I got you something." I opened and it was a pair of black leather lineman gloves. I loved those gloves, I kept them my whole high school career. They even begin to tear by my senior year, I just taped them up and kept playing. They made me feel invisible. That day at practice, to my surprise, everyone came with a new attitude and focus, we worked harder than we ever worked to get prepared for our next game.

Believe it or not, we started winning. I'm like okay, this thing is working. We were beating the best teams in the district. The coach got the whole team to believe in the goal, and promised us if we took it one game at a time and played at the level we were capable of we would win the district championship! The hardest game of the winning streak was the fifth game. It was against our crosstown rival Loyola High School. They were big, strong and fast. The had a running back that was so fast and so strong, if you didn't hit him low you were guaranteed to get run over. He was built like Mike Tyson but shorter and faster, that kid could run and hit hard. Their linemen were was strong and just was fast. Running into those guys I felt like I was hitting a brick wall. That game was so tough for us, but we pulled together and won. It wasn't a pretty win but we got the victory and were one step closer to our goal. Our coach did a great job at keeping us focused, he made sure we were all on the same page, taking one game at a time.

To achieve any goal or task it's important for you to know that you must envision it first in order for it to happen, and how you practice will become habit and if you are slack in preparing for whatever it is that you want, it will not come to pass. Now my dream that year was to score a touchdown in a game, being an offensive and defensive lineman there was no way they were going to give me the ball, so I knew if I was gonna score a touchdown I had to take the ball on defense and run it back for a touchdown. So before every game I would practice this play. I was the defensive end, the running back was going to run the ball to my side and I was going to hit him and he is going to drop the ball and I'm going to pick it up and run it back for the touchdown and I'm going to flip in the end-zone and do my dance. So before every game, I would practice this same play over and over. So much so that my teammates and coaches would ask me what I was doing, I said this what is going to happen, The running back is going to come around my side running the ball, I'm going to hit him, he's going to drop the ball and I'm going to run it back for a touchdown, then I'm going to flip in the end-zone and I'm going to do my dance. The laughed and told me I was crazy!

Game after game went by and it didn't happen, but we kept on winning so I was happy. Still, before every game, I would practice this. He's going to come around, I'm going to hit him, he's going to drop the ball and I'm going to run it back for a touchdown, then I'm going to flip in the end-zone and I'm going to do my dance..

The very last game of the year, the district championship game. Fourth quarter. The running back came running around to my side, I said aww...this is it. It was just like I envisioned it - he came running to my side, I hit him, he dropped the ball. I ran it back for a 70 yard touchdown, I flipped in the end-zone and did my dance. My teammates and coaches were on the sideline crying. Because what I envisioned, I manifested. They saw it come to pass and it brought tears to their eyes. We even got a penalty for my celebration dance, but we didn't care. We won the district championship after losing our first three games of the season! We were all so happy, we were jumping around, screaming #1, #1 Baby! We did it! We did it! We could wait to dump the Gatorade cooler on our coach's head. As I'm writing this I'm laughing but I feel bad for coach because it was the dead of winter in Chicago and we dumped a large cooler of Gatorade on his head and I know that had to suck for him, but he took it like a man, I must say.

At the beginning of my Sophomore year just before the start of football season, my dad came home and told the family we were moving to Virginia. He explained to us that my stepmother got a job offer in a small town in Virginia called Bristol. I was devastated. I had big plans of moving up to varsity with the rest of my teammates and going after another championship. The hardest thing I believe I ever had to do was tell my teammates and coaches that I was moving to Virginia. Some of my teammates and coaches even cried when they heard the news; it was a very sad time, we had just won the freshman district championship and here I was telling everyone I was moving, It hurt me deeply.

So my family and I packed up all of our belongings and moved to Virginia. We left all of our friends and family in Chicago and moved to a small country town where we knew no one. All I could think about on the plane ride was joining the football team. My dad takes me to the school and I get signed up and meet the coach. He tells me he's glad to have me part the team and to report to practice the next day at 3pm. That night I could hardly sleep I was so excited! The next day I report to practice and he doesn't even put me in. This went on for at least two weeks. I would go to practice and the coach wouldn't even let me participate! I so upset I went home crying every day. I told my dad "they don't even let me play in practice. I wish I could have stayed in Chicago, I was gonna start!" He said "Listen to me, you play football. I don't play football. If you want to play football, you've got to figure out how to do it. I don't have time to stop working, you calling me, you crying, because they won't let you play in practice, YOU have got to figure out how to make it happen, whenever they put you in at practice, whoever is in front of you, you take all of that frustration and anger out on him." And that is exactly what I did! The coach lined me up in front of this guy and I took all my pain and frustration out on him. BAM! I hit him so hard his chin strap came unbuckled. I want you to know, that guy is not my friend to this day. I put him flat on his back. They call that a pancake in football. I earned the respect of my new team after that one play.

From that practice on, I started every game. My junior year, I led the team in tackles and I got awarded defensive player of the year. I also was named to the All-City, All District & All Conference teams. My senior year I was in the best shape of my life, I put in a lot of work over the summer, I dropped a bunch of weight and added muscle I was ready to crack some heads. Here it is the first scrimmage of the year and I broke my foot. My dad takes me to the hospital and the doctor tells me they want to put a screw in my foot to mend the bone back together, I told that I didn't want to do it because I would miss too many games. I'm thankful to say I only missed the first two games and came back. My foot never really healed; I just had the trainer tape it up before each game and I played the rest of the year with a broken foot. I played middle linebacker and offensive guard. At the end of the year I led the team in tackles once again and got awarded the most valuable player award for the team. I was the first lineman in that school's history to ever do that. Right now I'm a part of that school's history. All because I did not give up. I made a decision to dig deep and keep fighting! I challenge you to Never Give Up and Go After Your Dreams!

Kelly Cole is a #1 Best Selling Author, Master Book Publishing Strategist & Speaker. Kelly has authored and published over 50+ paperback, audio and ebooks to date.

Kelly has been seen on NBC, FOX, ABC, The CW, Gospel Updates Magazine & more. As an consultant, Kelly has worked with clients who have appeared on OWN, Real Housewives of Atlanta, Bravo, NBA, WORD network, MTV, BET, Atlantic Records, and more. Kelly started Publishing Advantage Group 12 Years ago after quitting his day job at Wal-Mart, He almost ended up homeless but worked hard serving and helping other people's dreams come true, which ultimately led to his dream coming true of building a successful marketing & publishing company. In 2014 he was even elected into the GrindMoves Hall of Fame. He has been labeled a Business Guru for his knowledge and marketing wisdom that he has used to help people all over the world!

He is the proud father of three, a boy and two girls, and has been married for over 15 years to Natasha.

Contact Info:

Website: www.PublishingAdvantageGroup.com

Email: kelly@publishingadvantagegroup.com

Facebook, Twitter & Instagram: @mrkellycole

5 Success Principles So Powerful That Even An Aneurysm Couldn't Remove Them From My Brain

Jason Oman

My story is a bit crazy.

Have you ever heard of the book *Conversations With Millionaires?*

It was a #1 international bestseller, and I was blessed to have co-authored it.

Here's a picture of it just in case you're not familiar with it.

My name is Jason Oman.

After successfully launching multiple businesses, teaching authors how to get their books to #1 bestseller status, doing successful projects with more than 20 millionaires, and even being on TV; in 2007 I had a life-threatening medical condition.

I had Brain Aneurysm that almost ended me.

I ended up in a 10-day coma, with a 15% chance of survival. Luckily, it wasn't my time to go, and I still get to experience life with my loved ones every day.

One of the side effects of my aneurysm is that I often have some memory loss. But as severe as my medical condition is, it's not strong enough to remove from my mind the business success insights that I'm going to share with you today.

There are 5 Success Principles so powerful, that if you apply them to your business, you'll be head and shoulders above your competition.

I'm blessed to still be alive today to share them with you; so please, take them to heart.

Let's jump right into it…

SUCCESS PRINCIPLE #1: THE BEST SUCCESS FACTOR IS VALUE!

The more (and better) value your clients and customers experience from your products, services, & your whole business, the more they'll want to come back to get more of that great experience! And, the more likely they'll be to refer you to others, as well!

So, take the time to make sure you are adding and giving as MUCH value as you possibly can with each and every product, or service, you offer!

The better your customers, and/or clients feel about you, your products & services, and your business as a whole, the more and more successful you'll be!

So, make sure you invest some time and effort to work on maximizing these things as much as you possibly can!

It may even be a good idea to create a checklist of "items that add value" to remind you, and help you stay on top of various aspects of your business on an ongoing basis.

The bottom line is that the more time and effort you invest in adding value, the better and more successful your results will be!

So, make sure you do everything you can to make sure your customers feel like they should be paying more than they're paying for your products & services.

SUCCESS PRINCIPLE #2: DETERMINE YOUR REASONS WHY

When it comes to getting yourself to take the actions that lead to success, one of the factors that is extremely important is making sure you have enough of the RIGHT reasons to get yourself to take those actions!

So, if getting yourself to take enough of the right actions is a challenge for you, it might be incredibly helpful to work on thinking of (and even creating a list) with some more of the REASONS WHY you want what you want and more REASONS WHY you need to get yourself to take the right actions!

VERY few things have as much weight and control over your likelihood of taking consistent actions as the REASONS WHY you feel you need to take those actions!

If it helps, you can work on this by asking yourself WHY you want to achieve, accomplish, or get the things on your list of goals. Meaning, go through EACH goal on your list and figure out all the reasons you can think of that you want that thing.

They say that if you have a strong enough WHY, the HOW will figure itself out. and I know this to absolutely be true!

So, work on developing more REASONS to take the right actions to achieve the success you desire!

And, I'll see you in The Winner's Circle!

SUCCESS PRINCIPLE #3: CONCENTRATED MENTAL FOCUS

When it comes to making yourself as successful as you possibly can, there are a number of factors that are VITALLY IMPORTANT!

In fact, many of these factors have a direct correlation to some of the other factors that determine success as well! (Meaning they can create a synergistic effect where the combination of those factors takes things to an even MORE powerful level!)

So, I'd like to share, & reveal, one of the MOST important of ALL!!

It's really and truly, THE MOST POWERFUL & IMPORTANT FACTOR FOR SUCCESS

AND, best of all, it's something that YOU can benefit from and take advantage of for yourself as well!

(...Once you develop the ability to do it!)

The factor I'm talking about is something I call...

===> "Concentrated Mental Focus" <===

In fact, the degree that you can keep yourself focused on doing the RIGHT things consistently is the degree of success you'll achieve and enjoy!!!

So, anything you can do to give yourself this enormous advantage is something you should continuously and consistently work on doing! Even set up reminders around your home or work to make sure you're constantly reminded to work on this!

The bottom line, more than anything else is this...

The degree that you can keep yourself focused on doing the right things consistently and continuously will determine the level of success you ultimately achieve!

So, since this is among the MOST powerful and life-changing of ALL possible disciplines you can develop, it makes sense to set up reminders to help keep yourself focused on getting better and better and better at doing this on an ongoing basis!

MANY, many people have a challenge keeping themselves focused on the right things consistently. So, if you're one of those people then this is something YOU need to work on developing... and doing that NOW!

Best of all, the better you get at it, the easier and easier it is to keep yourself focused and on track on a continuous and consistent basis!

So, it's an ability that gets easier and easier and can bring you more and more benefits and results from doing it!

What more could you possibly ask for, right??

So, now the question becomes what do YOU need to do to get yourself to keep on track and focused on the right things consistently from today forward?

While it's fresh on your mind, go ahead and start making a list of things you can do to keep yourself focused on an ongoing basis!

This could be anything from cell phone calendar (or Google Calendar) reminders to Post It Notes on your Bathroom Mirror (To remind you while you brush your teeth, or get ready in the mornings). or anything else that can help remind you to stay focused on this consistently!

After all, until you develop the ability to keep and stay focused on the right things your chances of success and personal or professional growth are pretty limited and challenged!

So, it makes all the sense in the world to get yourself to do this ASAP - NOW!

And you may even want to remember who prompted you to do this to help get you focused and on track on an ongoing basis as well! :-)

After all, the more successful YOU become the more you can become an inspiration and catalyst to help others become more successful as well!!

SUCCESS PRINCIPLE #4: MINDSET…MINDSET…MINDSET

Next, I'm going to share a secret to success that many people never realize is an EXTREMELY IMPORTANT factor for creating incredible success for themselves!...

However, if you do discover, and then take action on this, the possibilities are truly UNLIMITED!

You see, what I'm talking about is the fact that unless you have your 'thinking/mindset' working in the right ways your chances for success are extremely limited & flat-out unlikely!

The point here is to realize the importance of making sure you take the right actions to get your mindset on track for creating incredible success!

Because when it comes right down to it, there is NOTHING as important as making sure you're thinking is on the right track if you want to create serious success for yourself!

So, the question is...

Are you consistently taking time to figure out what factors and elements of your own mindset need to be tweaked and improved so YOU can become as successful as you desire?

If not, maybe it's time to start doing that!?

If you want some help doing this, let me know, because I truly LOVE helping people break through any barriers that have been holding them back from the success they desire and deserve!

Because the difference between what you COULD be achieving and your current results might be EXTREMELY more intense than you ever thought?!?

But, with just a tiny little tweak or two, the difference it could make is truly AMAZING!

SUCCESS PRINCIPLE #5: BELIVE THAT YOU MATTER

After being able to personally meet a number of other highly successful entrepreneurs, one of the things I've discovered is that it's EXTREMELY important for you, or anyone wanting to be successful, to truly know and believe that you matter!

In other words, you need to realize, and believe in your gut, that YOU truly ARE valuable and deserving of success!

In fact, you are just as deserving, capable, and WORTHY of success as any of the people who have become incredible million-dollar level success stories!

Now, you may at first have some challenges hearing (reading) this. And if that's true then this message is THAT much MORE necessary for you to hear!

So, I just wanted to do my part to help you realize that you truly ARE someone who is capable and deserving of the success you desire!

So, keep staying focused and moving forward and I'll see YOU at the top, superstar!

Thanks for letting me be a positive factor in helping you make success happen!

After spending time with, & doing projects with more than 20 amazingly-successful self-made millionaires, I now enjoy helping others maximize their success, as well.

SUCCESS PRINCIPLE #6: WRITE DOWN YOUR GOALS

Ok, one last Success Strategy for you. Because, I believe in going the Extra Mile!...

Of all the things I've learned over the years, and from doing projects with a bunch of millionaires, there is one single concept that I consider to be among the most powerful. Not just because it's so simple & only takes a minute... But, also because of the amazing difference it can make in your life!

It's simply to start every work day, by writing out your most important goal to achieve that day. But, the real magic, and power clicks in when you actually write it out 20 times BY HAND!

Because, as you drill it into your mind, and memory, it'll become more and more of a solid focal point for your day.

You see, we all have at least 100 things every day that can distract us from making the magic happen in our lives. So, the better you get at keeping yourself focused, and on task, the more and more successful you can become. So, even though this is such a simple tactic, it can and will make an amazing difference in your life, if you truly take it seriously!

In fact, you can do this at any time each morning, and even while you're doing something as plain, and simple as waiting for your toast to get done in the toaster; or, while your car warms up, in the morning, etc.

So, take this truly serious, and make it a part of your morning disciplines. And, let's get you to the Winner's Circle, my friend.

Jason Oman / Featured TV Success Story. #1 Best-Selling Author of *Conversations with Millionaires*. My newest program is called **'Unlimited Income Streams'**. It contains the most powerful lessons, secrets, and even a step-by-step formula to launch new income streams whenever you want. It combines the most powerful lessons & secrets I learned from all the millionaires, and successful people I've been around over the years, especially, when it comes to generating new income streams whenever you want!

Note: I don't have a webpage set up for that yet as of the time of this writing. But, feel free to email me at Jason@JasonOman.com for more info on that. Just add a simple message of some kind, so I know what you're asking for.

THE HEART OF OUR FEAR

VALERIE DUVALL

I had been there so many times before. I possessed the drive, the intuition, the idea, and had the fire in my heart - I was an entrepreneur, and I was ready to take on the world.

Finally, I was ready for something better than what I was experiencing. My friends, my family—I knew they deserved better, and in my soul lived the energy to create that greater world for them.

My bright future was ahead of me. I was unstoppable.

But alongside the confidence and excitement it took to motivate myself to stand to the challenge, came a flood of doubt. The kind of doubt that makes you focus on every possible little thing that could go wrong and ultimately freezes you in your tracks.

That's where I found myself, over and over again, just stranded. My hopes and dreams floating away like puffs of smoke. Doubt leading me to believe that I was crazy to think there could ever be something more.

More times than I care to count, I have felt like that. And my entrepreneurial journey has been held back many times by doubt, indecision and fear.

Perhaps you are like me. Perhaps you have been disappointed to the point that you find it hard to keep going. Maybe your own fear has led you repeatedly to inaction and procrastination. But please don't despair and give up. Once you know the key that I am going to share with you, you will see that all is not lost.

There are plenty of experts out there ready and willing to give advice on conquering fear. I am certainly not alone. And I have heard many of these experts quote the old familiar saying by President Franklin Roosevelt, "You have nothing to fear but fear itself" - and I also know that statement to be true.

After all fear IS something you create yourself – in your own mind. So we should be able to control it and not let it hold us back – right?

But it isn't as easy as merely believing that fear is your own creation and that it doesn't need as much as a sideways glance from you. If it were that easy we would all just read those words and go about our merry way with fear in the rear-view mirror. But that isn't the reality, is it?

So, what is it then? Why does fear seem to take up so much space in our lives. What is the bigger truth keeping us stuck? There must be something more to it. There must be something down deep that we are afraid to lose.

Just what is at stake when we contemplate taking on exciting projects, or starting a new business? And just what are we protecting when we don't take on those same projects or procrastinate to the point of failure on the projects we do take on?

When we let fear win over we give fear its power, and let them manifest, as if they were in human form that could reach out with its own arms and pull out the rug from under us. That manifestation can be very scary and tricky to beat – but it can be beat.

I learned that we can beat down fear by understanding just what is at the root of that fear. And what I have come to believe is that ultimately, the root of our fear is tied up with the very thing that keeps us going, our dreams. And I believe it is the of possibility of having our very dreams slip away forever that binds us and makes us a slave to fear.

Those nagging thoughts that whisper or maybe shout "you aren't good enough," "you don't have what it takes," "you aren't smart enough," "you're lazy," keep coming into our minds. When we listen to those thoughts, we procrastinate, we hold back and we accomplish very little.

And here is the paradox. When we don't try the things we dream of, those dreams can stay there on a hill to be contemplated – to be admired. They remain something to look toward and something to hope for. If we risk going for those dreams, we risk the fact that we may fail and then never attain them. And somehow our dreams and hopes for a better future will be dashed - gone forever.

I think we all understand at our core - without hope, all is lost. So, there it is, we risk all! Scary indeed.

But here is the irony. If we do nothing, those dreams stay there, just dreams. But those dreams still breathe with possibility. Our hopes remain our beacon of light to hold onto.

But our brains and our emotions have played a cruel trick. The sad truth is that the very act of trying to preserve those dreams and keep them safe by avoiding and procrastinating, are the very actions that will keep us from ever attaining them.

Is all lost or is there a solution? How do we move forward with the worry that we will fail to attain our hopes and dreams, ultimately to never see the change we long for?

My answer is to stop "reaching" for those dreams. Now I know what you are thinking, but please hear me out.

I am not saying to stop having goals and to stop dreaming. That could not be further from the truth. As I said before, without hope, all is lost. As a matter of fact, I encourage you to make your dreams bigger! You can obtain things your mind cannot even imagine when you finally understand the basis for your fear and inaction and finally start moving toward your goals.

What I mean by "stop reaching" is to stop the endless grasping and clawing for what you want. This kind of frantic, anxiety ridden behavior leads you to make fear- based choices and to look for quick fixes or "get rich quick" schemes. Things that rarely, if ever, take you closer to your true path.

So, stop "reaching" for your dreams and start "living" toward them. Your life's dream is not some inanimate object to be grasped at. Make your dreams as much a part of your life as breathing and not just some list of things you want to obtain on a vision board.

Align all of your actions and decisions so that they move you on the path toward your dreams. There are only two paths on your journey. Every action you take in your life will lead you toward your goals and dreams - or away from them.

Now you may be thinking, "But Valerie… this is so much pressure! Every decision to be evaluated and dissected." But don't you see? When you start living your life in accordance with your dreams rather than just wishing, things begin to fall into place. But here is an important part that I don't want you to miss. Attaining your dreams is not a singular action. Nothing worth attaining is that simple. There will be many decisions to make and many actions to take. And as you travel on the road toward your dreams, there will be detours.

When the detours come, your path will adjust. No one failure will make or break you because you can pick up, change course and get back on the path instantly. When you experience success or failure – and there will be both – you will see just where your strengths lie. You will see what excites you – what motivates you. You will know what things to set aside.

So, when you see your path as a series of actions and decisions that will neither make or break you, but help you have a clearer picture of what you really want - the pressure is off. Fear can finally take a back seat. Even taking actions you know are not in line with your goals will ultimately help you to learn who you are – if you listen.

You are now free to chase after any dream knowing that there are no individual decisions or actions that will lead to ultimate failure.

Of course, you may fail. But failure is not final and will not crush your dreams. It is not an all or nothing proposition. Your dreams will adjust as you grow and become the person even you didn't know you could be – free of fear; free of loss of hope; and free to do whatever you want in life. You can obtain things your mind cannot even imagine when you finally understand, let go, and take deliberate actions toward your goals.   I'm rooting for you!

Valerie DuVall is a speaker, coach and product launch consultant who is sought after for her knowledge of the online sales process. She lives just outside NY City and works with clients around the globe. She takes a no-nonsense approach to working with people who seek motivational inspiration and want to take make lasting change. She can be reached at valerie.duvall@gmail.com

WTF Do I Do Now?

Anthony McCarthy

As I sat there, the letter in my hand, fighting back the tears, the only words running through my head were; "What The F**k Do I Do NOW?". Over and over as if the needle had stuck on an old vinyl record the phrase kept on repeating. But I had to get up and go meet my wife, as I approached her, I could see the happiness in her face, she said, "I have news" with a beaming smile, I answered, 'so have I.'

After 30 seconds of you go, no you go, she says: "I am pregnant (with child number 4!). I said that's wonderful and smiled from the bottom of my heart. After a few minutes of unreserved joy (well for an Irishman at least), my wife asks what my news is, " I have lost the business!".

That's just one of the many occasions where life has played its wicked joke on me and I believe it does that so we can recognise the good and appreciate the good.

Life is built to teach us lessons, sometimes we hear them, other times, well not so much. No one said life was going to be fair and well it has not been, however I love the sentence from one of the Rocky movies which says "It's not how hard you hit, but how hard you can get hit and keep moving forward".

My father has another saying that I cling to when the shit hits the fan, it's "loads of people in the graveyard, would love the problems you now have". Having laid my sister to rest when she was 30, as well as two nephews, I know this to be a fact. The intention of this chapter is not to get you feeling down.

I suppose what I am really saying is a problem is only as big a problem as we are willing to allow it be. I am not saying that this always works, far from it. However, it is the skill set that I have developed, through years of being knocked down and getting back up again.

It started in school. I went to a Christian brothers school and although I met some of the nicest and most Christian men that were Christian brothers, they were a few that were a stop below animals.

It now turns out that I am dyslexic, to some degree, (when I was in school, it was called being thick), so I still find it head bursting to spell some words.

Back when I was in school, the Christian Brothers still believed that the devil was in people who were left handed (I know - grown and educated men thinking that) I believe I should have been left handed when I write, but that was just not acceptable, when I was in school and in fact they would slap you with whatever was near if you were seen writing with your left hand so my writing to this day, is still awful. Thank god for the PC, otherwise I would be screwed.

Anyway one "brother", taught me technical drawing and metalwork. He was a monster in my eyes. In just one hour he hit me 228 times on the knuckles, with the blackboard eraser.

This man terrified me and every morning I would vomit before going to school. However during the 228 wraps on my knuckles and I always remember he would make you change hands for every 10, the first strike was the worse, after that he got into a bit of a rhythm.

During this particular session (of which they were a lot, however 228 was my record and it was for work missing, every bad letter etc. I was not disruptive or disrespectful in any way), something changed in me. I decided that I was going to be in control. I could not change the Christian brothers' behaviour, however I could control my reaction to it. So I stop grimacing, I stopped reacting and started looking out the window, winking at my friends in the class. This drove him nuts and he hit me harder, he was in a sweat when he was done after about 20 minutes. I could not move my fingers for the rest of the day. However I felt great.

I had stood up, in my own mind and said I will own how I feel. Now I am not saying that every now again the scared kid walking up the thousand mile road (well some days it felt like that) does not turn up. However, now I recognise it and control it. As I tell my kids, courage is not the absence of fear, it's moving forward even if you are scared to do so.

This has served me well in my business adventures and that and my father's saying (about the people in graveyards) are my cornerstones when I have needed them. At the start I told you about my first fall from grace in business, which in Ireland is like the kiss of death, a crazy situation I know but it is what it is. However when I closed the business, I was stuck into a lease for the building I could not get out of (now I could, however I am a different man today), so again I found myself asking WTF am I going to do now?

Having read all the business books etc., which say never give up, my advice on that is, never give up, however maybe you should change direction. Anyway, I went to Italy to one of the biggest kitchen and furniture manufactures and tied up the rights to distribute their products in Ireland.

We refitted the shop, financed by credit, and ran as a standalone for a short period. I brought in seven more shops around the country and gave the Cork shop to one of my old employees to run. We grew the business to £1.7m in 2 years. Life was great. Then, amazing news, we got the rights to distribute in the United Kingdom. We expected this to bring in around £7m a year.

Happy days.

So we lined up around 60 shops to go in the U.K.

I visited the Italian company's factory, which is the size of a large shopping mall, and I was a happy man as I flew back home to Ireland on a Wednesday morning.

On Thursday morning, my phone rang. I could see it was a friend of mine who was the distributor in Holland, that's weird, I thought, so I answer and Robert says: "Have you heard?",

I answer 'heard what?'

"They're gone, it's all gone!"

'What's gone,' I ask.

He goes on to explain that the factory has burned to the ground. Nothing left. Gone completely gone. Guess what I thought. WTF do I do now.

Now it can never be said that I am not stubborn, the universe is obviously telling me that the kitchen business is not for me, however I just did not hear it and went again, but this time bigger!.

I opened a 10,000 sq ft showroom and did projects all over the world, The USA, UK and some Islands off the coast of Africa. Go big or go home right.

Then going big happened, I won a contract for $6.5 million dollars, the single biggest sale I ever made. What's more I also have contracts in negotiation for over 60 million dollars. So I close the showroom and focus on the contracts I have and the new ones that are coming in.

Well the first contract gets delayed due to an internal dispute within the development company. In that time I met a guy called Matt Bacak at an event in Dublin and did his program, which changed my life forever, more about that in a bit.

Eventually the contract starts, yes and then there was a little crisis you may have heard of.

Called the financial crisis and property crash, pension funds go bang.

You guessed it, half-way through the contact, I can't get paid and I am in for a very large sum of money. Over $1 million dollars. I am back to WTF do I do NOW… Now we have five kids!

The good news this time is I was listening to the universe, you see I have always loved sales and marketing, I am now doing it for over three decades. Actually I am around long enough that, I know which a newspaper column is as wide as it is! (it's the distance your eye moves in your head, without turning your head. You see you pick a newspaper and sit down to read a book.

Well we used to, now we sit down to work on a pc or laptop and pick up a mobile device.) So when the big contract got delayed, I started internet marketing and loved it.

When I looked back over goals I had writing eight years prior, my main goal was to spend more time with my kids while they were growing up. One of my big regrets is that I missed so much in their lives due to business pressures.

Even on holidays I could never relax, never switch off. When I think about my time in the kitchen business, I loved design and sales and hated the rest of it. It was always arguing and I am just not good at arguing, I am fine with a row and we finish it and have a pint, however the construction industry is constant arguing. So now it's no surprise to me what happened and the person responsible was me.

That might seem strange when you consider I was to an extent a victim of circumstances, however I put myself in the position. No one else.

One of my greatest joys was being able to take my wife and five kids to Spain for six weeks on holidays. I worked for two hours in the mornings and we had a ball. Now I get to most of my kids matches and see them every day, as I built an office in my back garden and I am there if they want me.

My wife and I can carve out time for ourselves during the day, so we get to be a couple. The other great thing for me is that I have not worked a day in years. I do what I love, I help people get the life they want and I help business owners use the internet to make more sales.

It's amazing and an honour to go in and help people realise the power of the internet, which is only becoming more and more integrated into our world. Especially now with mobile. I have created mobile apps, online business and I am currently involved in a number of different projects, which keeps my mind occupied and always looking forward to tomorrow.

So if you are in a position of WTF do I DO now. Then here is what I recommend to you my friend. First grab a pen and paper, yes old school. Then vanish, go somewhere where you can be completely alone for a few hours, that's the hardest bit, when we are in this position, we want people to rescue us, I know I have been there. However the only one that will rescue you is yourself.

When you are in the quiet space, turn off the phone. Then sit down and list all the things that make you happy, what you love doing.

The answer to WTF do I do now is in that list. You just have to have the courage to chase it. I am not saying that it will be easy, I am not saying you will not fall, or have doubts. However, if you have the courage, you will succeed and that's the last piece of the puzzle, define what is success for you.. How? Well ask yourself this, If I have just three months left on this earth, what would I love to do. What legacy would that leave for my family and loved ones?

Life is precious my friend, don't waste a minute of it. My parting words are.

Learn from yesterday.

Do Today.

Plan for Tomorrow.

And no matter what happens, have fun!

If you would like to learn more about marketing online, go to http://irishmarketer.com   What can I say, once a salesman always a salesman.

Anthony Mc Carthy has never sat through a job interview in his life. At the age of 16 he started working as an independent contractor and partnered with his father to open a 10,000 sq ft tile business. He made his first large sale at 18, which was for over $650,000 and has been in sales and marketing for over three decades.

Anthony has owned and operated numerous business and is still a serial entrepreneur, with interests in a number of high tech companies.

He specialises in helping new or existing business people to succeed at what he calls "Digital integration", that's understanding how to integrate the online world into the offline world of sales. As a mobile marketing and online expert, who comes from a retail and sales background, Anthony is uniquely placed to merge the offline and online worlds to grow businesses.

As an international speaker, Anthony has helped thousands of individuals and business people, grow their online business. He is a husband and father of five, who gets to live out his dreams and passions on a daily basis.

For more on Anthony go to http://anthonymccarthy.com

WHITE WOLF

JENNY KAVANAGH

I have a voice in my head that wants me dead.

I am not the only one that has this voice- it's a very busy voice, it's out there taking over some of the best minds and characters that exist in our world.

I was an anxious, sad and bullied child who never felt like I could fit in anywhere. I remember always wanting to be anywhere else but where I was; I could be really looking forward to an occasion, then the day would arrive and I would want to be anywhere else but there!

I recognize this with hindsight, I just felt uncomfortable all of the time.

I was agitated, nervous, shy, scared or all of the above- and so I learned very early to mask all of that with a big personality, and later with make-up.

I think I shaped this persona on a number of people around me, but it constantly changed depending on my 'audience'. I would over compensate for what I thought I lacked and adjust accordingly to suit the company. I was a natural at it- a natural actor, and from a young age I loved performance- it was an escape from me.

When I landed a role in Fair City (Ireland's number one soap opera) I was elated. I loved my job, I loved the crew, the team and my fellow cast members- I was 16 years old and playing with the big boys!

They all taught me so much, I wanted to learn and I worked hard.

Being on TV in living rooms five times a week meant I was recognized regularly. Some people were kind but some nasty, even violent.

I was a teenager growing up as two people- one on screen, one off screen, but both of those people were being watched by the public.

I was too grateful for the opportunity to ever think about any negatives, I just accepted it was part of my job. I was right, only I didn't really *feel* that way.

I felt lost and scared and comments hurt me, but I had grown such a hard shell, there was little telling that those comments, looks, articles, demands or pictures were all getting to that little girl who never did get to fit in or feel accepted.

The 'constructed' version of me got on with the job that I really did enjoy so much: I was told where to stand, what to wear, how to sound, what to say, and when.

I was comfortable with that; it was being myself that I couldn't do. Most weeks I spent more time in character at work than I did as myself at home. Being alone was not something I wanted; I rarely spent time on my own and when I did there was a book or film involved so that the voice wouldn't get too loud to ignore. Five amazing years on that soap, and in those years I was in film, on stages all over the country, in TV dramas, some incredible events, helped some beautiful charities, met amazing people and wore some stunning dresses!

I was nominated for awards, I was on the covers of magazines- it was my dream come true.

I had been diagnosed with PTSD following a traumatic night when I was sexually assaulted- I told no one for almost 10 years and so leaving for London was to be a complete escape.

I was trying to escape myself though, and that was a problem- considering I was travelling with me! So when I got to London to pursue acting- I knew it would be tough, and that I would struggle. I didn't know I would be hungry, alone and after four years completely lost, mentally shattered and bruised on the side of a street, crying to come home.

I got a job in a bar, which meant I could go to castings during the day and work in the evenings, but that quickly became groundhog day.

I would go to work for 6pm, work a shift, have a couple of drinks after work to 'socialize', then trek across London for an hour on my own, late at night to get home.

I would wake up the next day at 12pm or 1pm, eat, shower and go back. My drinking very rapidly got out of control. I didn't see it, but the truth is I was more comfortable in my own skin when drinking. It took the pain away. The voice was silenced.

Relationships suffered- I pushed everyone away, I had no idea what was happening, or why everything seemed to be catching up with me.

My mind's 'delete button' stopped working- that place in my head I went to where nothing existed- that place where no thoughts, no pain and no fear lived, was gone too. I argued with people because I was angry, not at them- but with life.

I isolated myself, even though the last person I wanted to spend time with was me. The inner voice got louder and I crumbled.

I trudged through those dark days, alone, until a romance came to 'save me', or so I thought. But not before completely annihilating all that was left of me.

Two very damaged people who thought one could fix the other and neither could. It grew more and more toxic and abusive and eventually violent.

I was a shell, all that I saw were the bruises, and all that I heard was noise.

There was no remnant of the girl who adjusted to situations accordingly anymore, there was just a girl who woke up each morning and tried to survive the day.

That was what it had come to. I had absolutely no idea of who I was, and worse, no idea who I *wanted* to be.

As a teenager, I lost a very dear friend to suicide- I remember the confusion, the anger that he left, and the empty void that doesn't ever get filled by anyone else.

I was living in that empty void.

That inner voice was now 100 voices and they were screaming. I couldn't go on and I was genuinely convinced that no one needed me, no one loved me and I would be doing them a favour.

I was nothing, I was no more, I couldn't fake it anymore, I was lost, I was too broken to be mended.

I still feel some shame and guilt around the fact that I tried to take my own life; I think that comes from knowing now that I would have hurt a lot of people. At the time I truly did not feel or see that. That is how sick my mind was. Just like colds or flu, our heads get sick, but somehow we are conditioned to believe that makes us 'weird' or 'mad'. The *real* madness is that a cold or flu is a lot less likely to kill you than a sick mind. How dark it gets before the dawn.

There is a Cherokee legend- 'the tale of two wolves'- A grandfather explaining to his grandson of a fight between two wolves. One wolf is evil- he is pain, anger, envy, regret, greed, arrogance, self pity, lies, false pride, guilt, superiority and ego.

But the other wolf is good; he is love, joy, peace, hope, serenity, humility, kindness, benevolence, generosity, compassion, truth and faith.

The grandfather tells the boy that this fight is happening within him, and within all of us. The boy thinks for a moment and then asks- 'which wolf will win?'. The grandfather pauses, looks at him and answers, "The one you feed"

I learned how to feed the white wolf. Out of the darkness came a will and a drive to help, to live, to love. I have empathy and understanding, I have compassion and I am free from guilt and shame. I don't judge- because I stand in no position to, and I work on my humility, serenity and peace daily.

That inner voice, or evil wolf, is quieter- he is small and frail. I focus on the good, the color, the beauty and the possibility. Every day I exercise and I meditate, I eat well and I breath in the air that fills my body with energy and drive. I have passion and I have ambition. I qualified as a personal trainer and nutritional consultant, I moved to the south of France and built a life and business, and I get to help others change their lives and reach their goals. I see from a perspective of living now, not surviving, and I find so much joy. I can work anywhere in the world!

I have met the most incredible people and said goodbye to the relationships that were not serving me. Today I am the kind of human I can sit with, I can hang out with me, I can look me in the mirror and go to bed with me each night.

Because isn't that what it comes down to? That is peace: honesty within. I have beautiful friendships and relationships. I am living the adventure! I am not afraid to be wrong or fail anymore, what a relief!

What did I do to get from then to now? I asked for help.

I would not be here if I hadn't, and I wouldn't be continuing to grow if I didn't continue to reach my hand out for guidance. We don't have to have all of the answers- in fact life would be pretty monotonous if we did. New friends, and business partners have come into my life because I want to learn and grow.

At the moment, I am working with a herbalist in Ireland. Together, we will be launching a range of Green teas, supplements and health programs. This instant tea, hot or cold will combine flavor with herbal remedy. This is such an incredible thing to be involved in because we can genuinely help people on a practical level.

Change happens in a moment, it's the decision to change that takes time. Change is also inevitable, but the direction of change is where we often have a say.

What we consume, what we feed our minds and how we treat our bodies is something most of us have choice on, so to take our lives and bodies back is not only empowering; but rewarding beyond belief. When change is made- it's a process of little decisions. One small change daily- accumulates into a big change in one year.

All I have to think about is this moment, those choices, and living in this day.

And oh boy am I glad to be here today!

 **Jenny Kavanagh** is an award-nominated actress from Dublin, Ireland.

For almost a decade she has been involved in the personal health and fitness industry. Jenny is a qualified nutritional consultant and personal trainer with a passion for helping others achieve their 'best self'. Having been on a journey of self discovery and confidence building, she continues to educate herself and to offer more to those who want it. She has built her business 'Jenset Training' online and in the South of France, London and Dublin.

This year she has begun partnering with an Irish herbal company to create 'Instant Remetea' green tea blends with herbal remedies to help solve common ailments she and her clients face. Jenny's journey has given her a tremendous insight into the world of change and particularly health changes. Focusing on small steps and working with sustainable plans for her clients has been her cornerstone and she has seen the results in her clients.

'Every marathon starts with one step, and another, and another- so taking the first step with your hand in someone else's can be the guiding force that we need for change'

CHANGE OR DIE!

SEAN MCCARTHY

Change or die was a phrase that was coined in the mid noughties after the publication of Alan Deutshman's ground-breaking book, but I had that phrase in my head a couple of years before for a very different reason.

In the same week in 1998, I decided it was a good time to change careers (from sales administration to sports journalism), to move house and to have a first child.

I didn't realise at the time that my mechanisms for dealing with change were as poor as they were and how much each one of those was literally scaring the sh*t out of me. Having a first child is scary, I don't care what people say and not knowing what to do next is probably the scariest part.

I now understand how important mentoring is and while I wouldn't have called it that back at the turn of the century but my mother-in-law was a great mentor when it came to our first baby Sarah, the move to journalism was just as scary.

Gone were the rigid nine to five days and back then it was hard to get used to having less structure in the day. And moving house – we bought my wife's family home after my father in law died - and all the reconstruction work to convert part of the house into a granny flat for my mother in law were taking their toll on my health.

But being a *real* man, I was internalising it all instead of verbalising what I was feeling. The Crohns disease I was diagnosed with in 1999 after coming back from vacation from the US was as a result of poor diet but more importantly internalising a lot of sh*t – funny how our bodies will somatise (bring into our physical lives what our emotional lives are living) our feelings!

Like any other disease diagnosis, it was almost a relief to have a name put on it. Back before the Google machine was invented it meant researching by any means possible what caused the disease and what the prognosis for it was, and the prognosis was not great.

By 2001 I had totally handed over the control of my disease to somebody else (a specialist) and that specialist said to me by the end of that year that if I had another acute attack – I had been hospitalised for a couple of weeks twice in the previous three months - within three months that I would have to consider a bowel re-section.

My grandfather lived with us and I had watched him die from bowel cancer for four years when I was aged between 8 and 12 years of age so in my head even as soon as the word re-section was mentioned, my head immediately said 'No'.

As I walked back to my car, I just kept thinking 'I have to change or die'. It was that simple and that black and white.

That day I began a journey which has seen me to writing this chapter of a book.

Did I ever think back then that in 15 years time I would be free from the symptoms of Crohns Disease and off all medications for it. Again the answer is no because I was in a different headspace back then and headspace dictates everything that goes on in our lives.

It controls what motivates or demotivates us, what gives us courage to change or what makes us fear change.

I love Anthony McCarthy's saying of 'grab your two earlobes between your thumbs and forefingers and pull your head out of your own backside.'

Change in the early days didn't come easy when treating Crohns, but change never comes easy regardless of what it is you are trying to change.

And all change doesn't have to be as dramatic as Change or die but at the time I thought that phrase was true and what your mind can conceive and believe...

In a roundabout way via a great reflexologist and an equally good acupuncturist, I ended up attending a herbalist, Bridget Meagher, who helped facilitate the changes I needed to make in my life.

Diet change – away from irritating wheat and dairy – a bit more exercise (I had piled on stones due to the heavy dosages of corticosteroids and working on the top three inches of my body and how my brain dealt with the changes in my life began along with the medicinal effect of the herbs I was on, began to see changes happen in my life.

Small at first, but changes nonetheless, I could feel like I had more energy to deal with life. That and the self-empowerment that comes from taking charge back of your own health certainly had me feeling a lot different about my health and life.

One thing I will always be grateful to Bridget, was introducing me to green tea.

From the time I started drinking it and because now we had a thing called the internet and Wikipedia I was able to do a lot more research, I could see the benefits to general health as well as for helping to shift some fairly serious toxins from years of taking drugs for Crohns.

Given what my grandfather had gone through, the anti-cancer properties probably appealed to me as much as the fact that it was help me losing weight.

I was asking so many questions about the herbs during my herbal visits that one day Bridget – who had the patience to answer every one of those questions – handed me the prospectus for the International Register of Consultant Herbalists and Homeopaths.

It was there that I met Sandy and Marilyn Scott – two of the most amazing mentors you could meet, and both very different in their approach to mentoring. Sandy is a pragmatic man who worked on the top three inches by challenging my beliefs and used EFT (Emotional Freedom Technique) to change those old beliefs which were doing me no good.

Marilyn was idealistic, nurturing the positives that were already there and the new positives that were coming into my life.

In the whole Change or Die scenario mentors are hugely important for just making sure your head is in the right place, as I was to find out when I entered the world of business.

The family had grown to four children and as the web began to take over the commercial world, the newspaper I was working in and the newspaper industry as a whole began to feel the pinch.

Very few newspapers around the world adopted a Change or Die strategy, and as a result most of them are now dead or barely struggling to stay alive.

The world falling off the side of a cliff face in 2008 only added to the problem and even though financially it was difficult to complete my studies, I did so in 2010. As

I began to practice and see the positive steps I was helping people make, it gave me even more encouragement to stay on the complimentary therapy route.

I still stayed drinking all types of green tea and encouraging any patients to do likewise but when I asked any of them were they drinking it, it was always the same scrunched up nose as a reply from those who weren't drinking it. Most people couldn't take to the taste of green tea despite knowing how good it was for their heart health, mental health, for weight loss or for its cancer prevention. I did spend a lot of 2013 tasting and testing lots of different green teas both for myself and my patients.

I never really paid attention to the messages from God/universe I was getting during that time because my next Change or Die event was fast approaching.

In 2014, the newspaper I was working for needed to shed jobs by making workers redundant under a voluntary scheme. It was something I felt I had to take, I wasn't sure what the next step was but I knew it was time for change and I knew I wanted to be and was capable of being my own boss.

I was with a friend of mine, Pat Lynch, in his house one evening and he gave me a cup of green tea. The tea was the nicest I had tried and Pat informed me that the company that made the tea was Irish and was for sale.

I have reformulated the tea to make sure it is gluten free, non GMO and all products have been sourced through companies who value their ethics.

The company, Naturespharm, is beginning another Change or Die cycle currently. It has been available through pharmacies in Ireland, comes in an environmentally friendly glass jar so and is selling but the possibilities for expanding the range of teas and the benefits you can get from the teas is endless.

The change required is to go outside my comfort zone and look at white labelling and affiliate programmes and learning all about upselling so he will be an avid reader of a lot of other chapters in this book.

As I mentioned earlier, mentors are so critical when it comes to change.

I feel I am blessed with some of the mentors I have in my circle of influence including Anthony McCarthy, he understands change and if you read his chapter in this book you will understand why he understands it.

Good mentors will never make you change your mind per se, but they will ask you the tough questions and show you a road that you may need to travel.

Change is never easy but it certainly is easier than dying, whether that is in a physical sense, an emotional sense or a commercial sense.

If you have empowered yourself to walk the road and somebody with far more experience than you points out the route for you, then that road becomes easier to follow. I know that by making one simple decision in 2001 that I am where I am now and that was really a change or die scenario back then.

They are a bit less dramatic nowadays but the kernel of truth remains, unless you make that decision to change yourself, it will never be done and what I have learned from my journey is that the changes don't have to be dramatic in themselves, but the positive results can be.

Sean McCarthy (DBTh MIRCH) is a holistic herbalist who owns Naturespharm Ltd, a company that distributes a powdered green tea flavoured with herbal extracts. The company also distributes a vitamin B complex capsule which contains L Theanine and a Gluscosamine capsule which has ginger root powder as a natural anti-inflammatory.

Sean was diagnosed with Crohns disease in 1999 and has made a full recovery using a mind, body and spirit approach.

He was a rugby writer for a local newspaper before taking over Naturespharm.

He has seen the company go from strength to strength since he took over and is now ready to launch two new flavours of green tea as well as a supplement which will help with Urinary Tract Infections (UTI).

He knows that if he hadn't made a decision to change his life in 2001 that he may not be alive now. He can be contacted at sean@naturespharm.com facebook: naturespharm or www.naturespharm.com

THIS WAS IT

DARYL A. HILL

This was it, the last chance this midshipman (Mid) was standing tall in his military dress uniform in front of the admiral. If the admiral said yes, this midshipman would become a Marine, if no he would end up processed out serving in the Navy.

Firstly, it's important to note this was not a normal thing. Due to a string of events leading up to this moment and bad choices this Mid had landed himself into some pretty hot water. At this point he asked himself, "how did he even end up here or make it this far, put me out of my misery," definitely ran through his mind.

Why does this stuff always happen to me was running through his head. Literally every semester he was up again for being expelled from school for something.

It's one thing if this was just a one-time thing getting expelled, but every semester; this being the eighth and final semester could this Mid make it past this final hurdle. Every time it would be something slightly different and not enough to warrant being expelled. This time was different it was for conduct not academics.

Conduct is very black or white in the military. You either did it or you didn't. It's one of those things you can give away, and is very difficult to earn back.

It's often the intangibles about a person that make them unique and this Mid was no different.

Having the heart of a lion and the tenacity of the honey badger as demonstrated on so many occasions playing football against opponents, who on paper looked like a David vs Goliath matchup from the bible was the only reason this Mid had made it this far.

This no longer was about football though it was about becoming a leader of young men and women in the military.

The direct responsibility of someone's life where your decision could mean the difference between someone and even yourself perhaps, living or dying perhaps. These were much higher stakes than a game.

For the Mid it seemed like hours waiting outside the big wooden doors for the admiral's secretary to open the doors to go in. When you go to school at the Naval Academy it's not college. It's a military school with rules and regulations that a normal college or university simply does not have.

There is a rule book the size of the old school thick yellow pages telephone book and there's even a catch all rule that says "Unbecoming of an officer,"

Who interrupts that you might ask?

That is left up to the officers appointed by the president of the United States for this young Mid. The real question the admiral wants answered is what type of leader will this young Mid be to future sailors and marines.

When in a leadership position, it's vital to know how to lead and in order to do that you have to be a great follower first.

What makes a great follower is simply do your job to the best of your abilities and be accountable for it. When you go outside of your expertise or do other people's jobs then you are not focused on what you have to accomplish.

It's then, whether on the football field or the battlefield, that assignments get missed and people make mistakes that cost games and lives in combat.

Pause for a moment and write down your definition of leadership and remember there is no wrong answer.

Leadership:_____

_____

Now if you asked a room full of people to write down their definition of leadership you'd very quickly realize everyone has their own definition.

I'm going to share with you a couple very successful organizations definitions of leadership.

Bill Belichick Five Time Super Bowl champion and New England Patriots head coach defines positive leadership based on two things:

"Positive leadership, in my mind, comes from two things: No. 1, doing your job. If you don't do your job, I don't see how you can give any leadership. A lot of people who aren't very good at doing their job, and who try to give leadership, are just looked at as 'Look, buddy, why don't you just do your job? Why don't we start with that instead of trying to tell everybody else what to do?' So No. 1 [is] do your job. No. 2 [is] put the team first. If those two things are in place, then that person is going to give positive leadership to the team."

Where did Bill learn leadership? For starters he grew up on the United States Naval Academy where his father Stephen Belichick coached for over 30 years. Bill quickly became obsessed with football.

At five, he sat on the family porch and listened to Navy assistant coaches talking football. At six, he memorized Navy's plays. At nine, he went to the weekly meetings, where his father gave scouting reports to the players.

At 10, instead of doing homework, he analyzed film and diagrammed plays. At 12, he and his father drew up offensive plays, then created defenses to stop them. It's no coincidence based on how he was raised on how he leads and why he has more Super Bowls than any other coach in NFL history.

His dad was also known for ruling with an iron fist when it came to conditioning and off season workouts. Zero tolerance and excuses, I mean here is a guy who joined the Navy during World War two and served as a Naval Officer in Normandy and Okinawa.

Stephen knew what it was to also be accountable and put the team first as he had done this for his country serving in World War Two. He knew what these young Midshipman were up against upon graduation. They would soon be leading sailors and marines in combat. The philosophy, the more you bleed in peacetime the less you bleed in battle is something the Navy coach knew all too well.

Now there is this organization called the United States Marine Corps and they know a thing or two on leadership.

This is the Marine Corps definition:

"The official Marine Corps ebsite defines the leadership traits in the following manner: BEARING is the way you conduct and carry yourself. Your manner should reflect alertness, competence, confidence, and control. COURAGE is what allows you to remain calm while recognizing fear."

If you were to read between the lines it says, "staying calm under fire from the enemy that wants to kill you, before you kill them in order to give the order to your Marines to kill them." And to shorten it further, "to have the ability to inspire others past what they think is even possible." That is what leaders do every day. They provide the vision that is so big other's dreams are able to fit inside of it.

In life, business or battle it's the leader who inspires people through their vision and gets the buy in from the team that has the most success in life. It's the difference between being great and what legends are made out of, where their stories are to be passed down through generations.

Take a look at what the founding fathers of America did they willingly signed a death certificate now known as the United States Declaration of Independence, where which had the United States lost the revolutionary war against England they surely all would be hanged.

They stood up and spoke for their people from 13 individual colonies saying no more. Amongst these men a general was appointed in charge of the Army that would eventually defeat the British.

George Washington would lead his military against all odds crossing the Delaware River in the middle of winter, to defeat the British in two battles which would gain the momentum that led to victory against England. That's why he is a legend and known as the "Father of the country (USA)."

The type of leader you are in your life, organization, company or household will determine how you inspire yourself and others. It doesn't matter if you are a loud leader or a soft leader, for leadership is ACTION not words. A valuable lesson is watch what others do, not what they say because there are a lot of people out there putting out hot air or like to motivate others.

In combat you never ask your sailors and Marines to do something you would not do yourself. You always put yourself in the most dangerous points of friction in the battle because it's at these times leaders either win or lose the battle.

In football it's no different during the Super Bowl coach Belichick got the ball in the hands of his leaders and the defense in the best position to make plays that allowed them to come back and win, when sports announcers had already gone to bed posting on social media congratulating the other team. It's the leaders who tell you they are doing the undoable stay out of their way. They are the ones who inspire others.

The big wooden doors opened and there the admiral sat behind a large oak desk. The Mid marched in and reported in at attention in full military fashion. Palms of the Mids hands were sweating and he was not asked to sit down and chat he stood at full attention standing straight up tall as the admiral asked him about why he should allow him to graduate.

The answer was a simple one, "Sir, I want to serve my country as an officer in the United States Marines, Sir!"

The Admiral drilled him on what had happened and how he ended up in his office. The Admiral knew this Mid had the Honor, Courage and Commitment in the face of adversity and knew that is what would make him a great officer of marines. The question the admiral really had was does this Mid understand that he has those qualities and was he ready to stand tall in front of Marines as a second Lieutenant in the US Marines.

Still the Mid did not know if he was getting sent home or to graduation but, he knew in the next few minutes it would all be over one way or another. There is no script to meetings like these and it's based on the Officer's decision. There is no appeal or reconsideration this was it.

Sweating and remaining as still as possible this Mid was hanging on every word the admiral said with only sixty days until graduation after four and a half years to get to this point hanging in the balance. The Mid began thinking about how proud family and friends were at all the accomplishments from playing college football to about to become a graduate of the United States Naval Academy and serve as a marine, everything hung in the balance.

And then it came, "Midshipman Hill I'll make a deal with you keep out of trouble and serve your restriction time out because I look forward to seeing you in those second Lieutenant bars serving Marines."

Daryl A. Hill, US Marine Infantry Veteran, is the creator of the Money Blocks System used to find out why you are leaving massive amounts of business revenue on the table. He primarily works with entrepreneurial wounded sheepdogs who have been affected by Business PTSD. If you are an entrepreneur that desires to reach the next level in income head over to www.DarylHill.com to take a five-minute quiz to find out what is keeping you from your income goal.

THE END?

JASON MYERS

The End? Yes, the end. I decided to start this with the end. So, there you go.

You can stop reading now.

If you're still reading, it tells me you're a little different.

Great.

Now, let's discuss the two types of "end" I want to address before we get into the thick of this book.

First, is the "hurdle end". You see, most people stop before they ever get started. Maybe it's a due to a small bit of friction, hardship or doubt. A hurdle stops them in their tracks. Let's dive into this and take a look at a typical scenario this book strives to address.

Suppose for a moment you have an idea for a business. Even if you're not, bear with me for a minute. Imagine you have this business idea. You're fired up, can't sleep and can't think about anything else. The pressure inside you is building to the point where you finally and abruptly spew the idea all over family and friends. It is likely akin to projectile vomiting your idea all over them.

While your family loves you and your friends love you, they've heard it before. In fact, you've probably even been pitched an idea by one of them!

This is typically the beginning of the end. Sadly, family and friend resistance is the leading cause of the early demise of so many successful entrepreneurs. Many die before they grow wings.

I was extremely lucky as a kid and into adulthood to have parents who had a bit of an entrepreneurial streak and so they always supported whatever I was "into" at the time.

Most of my friends growing up did not have this benefit.

The second type of "end" is that you should always begin with. In other words you must have "it" in mind. Yes, begin with the "end" in mind. While it sounds simple, it requires some careful and thoughtful planning, adjustment and effort.

To focus on the "end" seems to be in direct conflict with focusing on getting started. That is until you see that the beginning is the end and the end is the beginning.

If you take nothing from our time together, stuff this nugget in your pocket and hang onto it like an ounce of gold. In order to achieve that which you want, you need to have a solid picture of where you want to end up.

You need to spend some time crystalizing the vision of where your efforts will take you. This is the nucleus of the lifestyle component of the Formula. I cover this Formula in depth in my book series called Independent Wealth Formula and we teach its principals at the IndependentWealthInstitute.org. You see, the reason I felt compelled to write those books and this chapter was to help people align their entrepreneurial and/or work efforts to their ideal lifestyle.

How many people do you know who are miserable in their work or business lives?

I bet it is more than you first thought. If you don't know anyone in this misery boat, I would buy a lottery ticket because you are an anomaly. Seriously, this is one of the largest issues facing business owners and entrepreneurs.

As a serial entrepreneur myself, I find that most employees who work for Da Man, are miserable. I also find that most business owners are not living their ideal life. I find that entrepreneurs are closer to the Holy Grail than the aforementioned people.

Why is this?

To me there is a distinct difference between a business owner and an entrepreneur. One thing first, before I get hate letters about being anti-employment. This can apply to an employee situation too, it is just easier to plan your life if you have some semblance of control. As an employee you are on their ship, you are not commanding you own, unless you take an attitude of free agent to the job.

My premise is to design your life now and live it now and become independently wealthy sooner rather than later. Sound good? Good, read on…

An entrepreneur is an opportunity seeker, a capitalist and a perpetual or serial creator of revenue streams. A business owner is married to a business (a.k.a., job). An employee is simply a resource leveraged by a business to get a job done in exchange at a positive return on cost - money for hours or money for results.

This hierarchy of sorts: Entrepreneur, Business Owner and employee typically follow a lifestyle freedom curve along these lines: Liberated, Shackled and Controlled. Entrepreneurs are liberated because they have several independent income streams.

Business owners are shackled to their business because they are the most important person in daily operations. Yes, the old ball and chain is the business not a spouse.

Professionals suffer from the shackle syndrome too. Doctors, Lawyers and Accountants each have this issue of being the source of the revenue and when they are not at work they make no money.

Employees are simply controlled by their boss and the machine and ironically, they have more freedom that a business owner. Especially, as it comes to time off, vacation and the ability to "punch-out" or "unplug" at the end of the day and they can often "forget" the J.O.B. until the next day.

Business owners are typically shackled to their operation before, during and after all operating hours and cannot "punch-out" to really enjoy life on their terms.

Entrepreneurs, however, are able to dance between the revenue sources and make the best use of their time to maximize the return on invested time.

Which one of these is for you? I presume that if you were attracted to this book that you must be desirous of the entrepreneur type lifestyle over the others. If you're an employee, at least now you know that you can become a free agent. I would say that would serve as your gateway attitude to a more liberated entrepreneurial lifestyle.

The Formula is based on the concept of creating entrepreneurial pursuits that fuel your ideal lifestyle while avoiding the shackle syndrome.

To this end (pardon the pun), the end is the lifestyle. The end is the beginning, to an amazing life.

The Formula is a system, framework, mindset and a blueprint to design your ideal lifestyle. In order to do this, you need to have a crystal clear idea of what that lifestyle should look like.

I wouldn't dare impose my personal ideal lifestyle upon you, as we are all individuals. I think you would agree there are no "right" or "wrong" lifestyles.

There is only the lifestyle that is "right" for you. As a result, I must impress upon you the importance of spending some time exploring the far reaches of your desires.

What's at risk should you not implement the Independent Wealth Formula?

You might start a business or buy a franchise only to wake up years later realizing that you are a prisoner to it and cannot enjoy your life. Life is simply too short for that nonsense. If you happen to be an employee looking for inspiration to take the leap to entrepreneurism, you could continue your path or spend some time soul searching for the ideal lifestyle and then leap towards the entrepreneurial pursuits to achieve that life.

It is best to **visualize** the end result – the lifestyle.

Before we continue, it is important to mention a critical point. You bought this book. That places you in an elite group of people who take action. Then there is a group inside of the buyers group who will follow up and take more action. I call this the 1% group. 1%'ers are those who will have their ideal lifestyle and as a result will enjoy true independent wealth. Are you a 1%'er?   Let's work on your vision…

From this point forward, I am totally going to dismiss any nonsense of single business ownership or employment. I am going to assume you are drawn towards the entrepreneurial lifestyle. A lifestyle of freedom to create, live and enjoy the fruits afforded by the successes you have had and will have. A lifestyle that is not beholden to one source of income or tied to one business.

So you might be thinking, "That's great, but how do I determine my ideal lifestyle?" Let's do a couple exercises. We'll start with this exercise:

My Perfect Day

I want you to list out a perfect day for you from the moment you wake up to the point where you enter the bedroom at the end of the perfect day.

This is not an exercise to design the typical day. No, it is to design the perfect day.

Example:

5:00AM – Breakfast Smoothie

6:00AM – Meditation/Exercise

7:30AM – Shower/Hygiene

8:30AM – Planning Day

9:30AM – Trading

11:30AM – Lunch w/ Someone Important (Family/Friends)

1:00PM – New business ideas

2:30PM – Snack/Existing Business Review

4:00PM – Bike riding, Kite Surfing

6:00PM – Dinner with Friends/Family

8:00PM – Research/Reading

Now, this is obviously a sample perfect day. It tells us a great deal about the person though. Let's analyze what it tells us about the person.

Personal Lifestyle Priorities:

- Early to Rise
- Fitness
- Organized/Disciplined
- Investment Oriented
- 1 and ½ hours on existing businesses
- 1 and ½ hours on new businesses
- Family/Friends meals

From a business perspective, you'll notice that there are three hours split between new and existing businesses. Then there are two hours on investing or trading (Wealth Management).

I don't know about you, but I think most people would like to have several hours for family and a few hours to keep the revenue coming in while still having the opportunity to exercise. For me, this beats a 16 hour workday, fast food on the run and no time for family or anything else.

I can throw a dart at nearly any business in the phone book to deliver a grind of a life for you. If on the other hand, you prefer to make as much money, but with less invested time, then you need to deliberately make some decisions to allow the lifestyle to develop.

The best way to achieve the ideal lifestyle is to live the perfect day as many days of your life as possible. Some days, life gets in the way of lifestyle. However, the more you live your ideal day the closer you will get to your goal.

So, let's look at the end lifestyle goal that the previous perfect day can manifest for you:

The Ideal Lifestyle

By stringing a long series of the perfect days together, you can achieve the lifestyle you desire. A quick review of the components of the day will help us see the bigger picture:

Personal Lifestyle Priorities:

- Early to Rise
- Fitness
- Organized/Discipline
- Investment Oriented
- 1 and ½ hours on existing businesses
- 1 and ½ hours on new businesses
- Family meals

So, these priorities if achieved more often than **not** would create the following broad themes in a lifestyle:

- Great Health

- Efficient Success

- Income from Multiple Independent Sources

- Great Family time

I don't know about you, but the list above sure beats a 9-5 grind and being sick and tired of being sick and tired.

The final piece of the lifestyle design process is to take a yearlong view. Here is how I do it. I created an online calendar using Google. This calendar I use to hold all desirable events. I use this plethora of events to keep me focused on doing more of the things I want to do.

A funny thing happens when you occupy your time doing things you want to do, things you don't want to do just don't happen.

You see, the strategy of filling a calendar with intentions of events is to create a long term lifestyle map of things to do.

In my calendar I have stuff every week taking place all over the world. I have schedule conflicts among these intention dates and the other "stuff" on my regular calendar.

Absolute and sheer joy occurs when I move an item from the intention calendar to the commitment calendar. Do I miss most intention items? Absolutely. But, it serves to keep me focused on doing more of them and less of the things that just don't matter.

Go ahead; create a lifestyle map by mapping your ideal day and a yearlong intention calendar today. These simple shifts can change your life.

Drop me a line and let me know how these ideas impact your life.

 **Jason Myers** is a pilot, inventor, serial and parallel entrepreneur, international speaker and best-selling author, and perpetual sponge for knowledge. He has started, invested in and sold many successful offline and online companies since 1991. He is often referred to as a business ninja with a swiss army knife, able to diagnose and fix nearly any issue. Growing businesses with effective marketing and operations is a passion of his.

Jason enjoys mentoring entrepreneurs on creating their ideal lifestyle and in making business their servant. He is Co-founder of CXO Collective International, a Private Equity firm with 20 companies and a non-profit Global Entrepreneurial organization that harnesses the triad of: Capital, Talent and Opportunities. CXO focuses on acquiring stakes in companies and growing them for fun and profit. CXO Collective has grown to attract members in 38 U.S. states and 10 countries. Members can earn performance based stock/equity/cash incentives compensation in the form of consulting fees and stock. To join the movement, head on over to http://www.cxocollective.com/heros (to get free membership, a $3,500 value)

You can also contact Jason directly on Facebook at facebook.com/jasonmyerscxo or on Linkedin https://www.linkedin.com/in/myjason or via email at: jason.myers@cxocollective.com (no spam please)

THE USELESS TREE

NICK JAMES

Two men were lost. They were walking along trying to find their path back to the car and they were very hungry. The sun was hot and it became almost too hot to go any further, this made the men very grumpy. They spotted a single tree in the distance and decided to go and rest under it and take shade from the hot day.

Gazing up into the branches, one man said to the other, "What a useless tree this is. Look at it! We come across a single tree and nothing else all day and it does not have fruit or nuts that we can eat, and we cannot even use its wood for anything because it is so soft."

"Don't be so ungrateful," said the other man. "The tree is being extremely useful to you at this very moment, shielding you from the hot sun."

This is a simple but powerful testimony that moment to moment everything is serving us. Even if we do not realize it, everything has a purpose for us – big and small.

If last month, you had to shut a business down or sink a project – instead of yelling at the closed door, look ahead and see that there is a window opening. I believe that we can use everything, even the seemingly 'useless' events of our lives.

That ignorant customer teaches us patience and perspective, that terrible investment teaches us that we can pull through anything and still bounce back.

Maybe it saved us from a huge disappointment even further down the line. We don't know the reasons for things until we look back in hindsight. Sometimes that hindsight comes years after, but we soon understand that everything in life is usable and positive.

The trick is to see it that way, otherwise you will overlook the current benefits that your disappointments have offered you. Ask yourself what you can learn from these events instead of cursing them. Ask yourself also how you can use these learnings to push you forward, either in business, as a person or in your personal relationships. There is always an upside; that is how it works. To really see it, you must do what everyone else is not doing, that is saying 'thank you' to your failures. They are your greatest teachers and protectors when you look back. Decide to see it for what it may be now, instead of waiting those years to look back.

I promise you, when you see all of life as if it is for you and not against you, it will be.

Nick James was recently named 'Marketer of the Year' by Marketing Guru Matt Bacak.

Nick is also widely recognized as the United Kingdom's premier coach for anyone wanting to break from the 9-5 grind and to start a highly profitable home-based Internet business instead.

Having struggled with Dyslexia since childhood and leaving school with low grades and self-esteem, Nick found himself bouncing along the poverty line and struggling to hold down mundane jobs. However his life turned around quickly when a customer loaned him a self-help book. Within 6 weeks Nick became a completely different person, buying and listening to as many courses as he could from experts like Brian Tracy, Bob Proctor, Jack Canfield & Mark Victor Hanson. This new learning gave Nick the confidence to set himself up in business.

Since registering his first domain, Nick has gone on to publish hundreds of websites and sell over $11 million dollars worth of products and services online. During that time Nick has also created various manuals and courses to explain each of the steps he's taken.

If you've ever dreamed of running your own high-profit Internet business, then you're invited to enroll into a free 7 day eClass to discover the strategies Nick uses to run his two successful million dollar a year home-based businesses.

OTHERS HAVE GOOD INTENTIONS JUST LIKE YOU

WARREN WHITLOCK

In the 40 years I've been studying self-improvement I've seen this principle proven time and time again.

I've been most successful myself when I find out what other people want and then get it for them. When I need to find new customers, improve sales, sell an idea, or even help a family member, I have found that it's much easier to focus on serving the needs of that prospect, client, friend, or relative.

I learn their core desires, then I try to make sure that those desires are filled. One way or another, my needs are always taken care of.

The Law of Reciprocity states that once you give something to someone, they are far more likely to respond favorably to you. Usually, you'll get what you need from the same relationship you build by giving. Other times, you give and don't see a quick return, but sooner or later, often in ways you'd never expect, it all balances out.

I've made giving my mantra, my core philosophy. On occasion, I still have a bad day, worrying about my problems, screaming to get my own needs filled. Focusing on yourself is hard work. It is much easier to focus on others. You'll get better results and have a lot more fun.

Giving has always worked for me. The moment I switch my focus from myself, options open up, and it's easier to solve any problem or obtain any goal.

It's as simple as this: stop focusing on yourself. We were taught to set goals, focus on achievement, develop good habits, and strive to improve ourselves to get the best results. It's true, when you're motivated, anything is possible. Striving, pushing, struggling, and working hard will get results. You will achieve your goals and likely some negative side effects. Hard work will get you somewhere . . . but where? Sometimes, you'll wind up learning that you were working on the wrong goal.

If you use this universal principle and switch your focus to getting other people what they want, you'll find that you always end up with what you want . . . with a lot less struggle. Things just work out.

Billionaires know this. More than one has taught this simple formula for success:

Find out what people want

Get it for them.

The natural outcome of focusing on yourself will usually leave you selfish—putting yourself before others. We don't mean to be self-centered, but when we think about our own desires, that's what happens.

We're bombarded today with news reports and political rhetoric that feels like everything is us against them.

Truth is, most of us are more alike than different. When we drop the pretense that they are the enemy and expect people to be good, they usually are. We may oppose their issue or group agenda, but real individuals are usually nice people when you get to know them.

The best example I've seen recently is the Polarity Partnership that worked in Charleston, South Carolina to make positive progress after a troubled young man open fire and killed nine people in a church.

In the documentary From Tragedy to Trust, you can see how police, government, religious and civic groups were invited to sit down and have a discussion about what they had in common and find a way forward.

When we accept others, listen to their authentic desires and let go of the differences, we learn that we are mostly headed in the same direction, and giving our help and support to the good is always more productive than fighting.

With the best of intentions, a person of integrity tries to be fair, to establish a quid pro quo, where he balances what he can get with what he gives. "I'll scratch your back if you scratch mine." That's a fair, honest way to do business . . . but there is something better.

It's Better to Give Than to Receive

From the Golden Rule through all great spiritual teachings we are encouraged to give, to be charitable.

No mention is given of quid pro quo. We are instructed to give service without seeking a reward, not to "give unto others if they give unto you." Give up the struggle for quid pro quo, and you'll unleash the power of the Law of Reciprocity.

It's more than a moral or religious teaching. It's just good marketing sense.

In Influence: In The Psychology of Persuasion, Robert Cialdini describes an experiment where a person is put in a room for a research experiment, not knowing that the other person (Joe) performing the same task is, in fact, the researcher's assistant.

Joe leaves the room during a rest period and returns with two sodas, giving one to the research subject. Later, the subject is asked for a small favor: Joe needs to sell some raffle tickets. The study concluded that Joe would sell twice as many tickets to subjects that had received the coke—a 200% improvement when a small gift was given.

We know that samples, gifts, and promotional items increase sales, but there's a bigger point here. Would Joe have doubled his sales if he had brought in the soda and said, "I'll give you this if you buy tickets"? Probably not.

I've used the power of giving at my Ochen.com website. We give away dozens of gifts during our promotions, all provided by people who have learned the power of the Law of Reciprocity. If you have a sample of true value, you can give it away to let people learn about what you do. Thanks to the Internet, there is no cost to being generous.

Giving something with the expectation of an immediate return works, but giving a real gift, forgetting your needs and focusing on what other people want, will give you a much better return. The universe will not stay out of balance.

You will get everything you desire and more. All you have to do is give, and the Law of Reciprocity will always pay.

True joy comes from love and service to others, so follow the billionaire's advice, find out what people want, and see that they get it. You'll feel great, and you'll always get back more than you give.

Find out what people want and see that they get it. It's as simple as that.

Warren Whitlock is an influence architect. In 2008, he wrote the first book about Twitter and Mobile Marketing, later the bestselling "Profitable Social Media: Business Results Without Playing Games."

He is the host of Social Media Radio and speaks frequently about social media marketing, online publicity and marketing, social networking and building lifetime value for rapid growth.

Warren helps businesses transform to a new way of doing business using social media and online marketing and promotion to attract the right audience from the billions of people using the Internet.

His breakthrough strategies to integrate mobile marketing, public relations and lead generation with conversions to return on investment for lifetime value has helped thousands of businesses achieve rapid and continuing results from improving their marketing process.

Warren has worked in technology, business services, broadcasting and is currently involved with media, health and other startups. He is the Director of Startup Grind Las Vegas and on the board of Conscious Capitalism. He's known on social media sites as @WarrenWhitlock, where you can find him having individual discussions and answering questions daily.

BECOME A BRANDED EXPERT AND SHOW YOUR AUTHORITY

C. Mike Lewis

In today's marketplace, you need to be THE expert in your field. It's imperative that the public knows, likes and trusts you. So, what's the best way to get potential clients to come on board with you? Through Branding.

Your brand is communicated through everything you do – from your name to your logo and slogan to your design theme. Whatever you use to promote a product or service is part of your branding.Everything your company does is communicated through your brand. It illustrates just who you are and exactly what you do, shows your worth, and distances you from your competitors.

But before you can truly convey your brand, you need to know how your company is perceived by your adoring public. How do they really see you? Do they see you as arrogant or aggressive? Are you approachable, modest and humble? Or are they so confused that they just don't know who you are?

Keep in mind that a brand is not a tangible item. It doesn't exist in our world. So, why is branding so important? Because it exists in our customer's minds. Just put yourself in their shoes. When you go looking for a company to do business with, how do you choose? Do you like their logo? Do you like what they have to say on their website? Do you check out their reviews first? How do you first feel about them? Why do you want to buy from them and not their competitor?

For many, many years my mother-in-law always wanted to own a Lincoln. Why? It was perceived as luxury. Wealth. It meant that you made it in the world. You were somebody. So why did she feel a Lincoln was better than a Cadillac? Perception. Television commercials showed the cars outside of million dollar homes, at the fanciest restaurants, at the Met. When you went to their showroom it was glamourous and pristine and "smelled like money." Are Lincoln's better? My mother-in-law thought so.

Just as with the Lincoln, in order for good branding to work you have to have Perception, Consistency, and Attitude. These are qualities that endear people to you. They want the exact same message every single time they come in contact with your website, with your social media pages, with your brick and mortar storefront, and with you. Don't be funny and whimsical on Twitter, and then gruff and solemn on Facebook. Your customers won't know who you are, so they won't want to do business with you. A seamless user experience is what they want, and that is why they will choose you.

Credibility

Branding comes in all forms, and credibility is a huge part of the equation. Before people learn to trust you, you have to be credible. Before you can create credibility as an expert, you have to understand what it is and what isn't.

Let's say you're a blogger and post that it's only a 6-hour flight to New Zealand from Texas, or in Florida it never gets below 79 degrees. Both are false statements; therefore, your credibility is gone.

I know I might ruffle a few feathers here, but I just don't understand how a twenty-one-year-old can call themselves a Life Coach. They haven't even experienced life yet! They haven't been out in the world long enough to know what business is, what works, what doesn't work, and more importantly, who they are. Unless you're one of the rare few who've been extremely privileged, I don't feel you have anything to offer me.

But a forty-year-old who's been around the block a few times, worked in the business, had or has a few successful businesses of their own, has a good following and is well-known with positive results, this is the type of person that I deem credible.

Here are a few ways to make yourself credible, while branding your business:

- Be Professional
- Always focus on your client or customer
- Pay attention to details
- Always look for a way to take things one step further

- Create a Social Media Page
- Become a part of your fans' everyday life
- Answer simple customer service questions
- This will build confidence in you for potential customers
- Create a Membership for your Site.

  This will demonstrate your expertise
- Anticipate & deal with issues you've come across in your professional life
- Reassure your customers that you know what they need
- Provide Contact Information
- Prove you're a real person
- Make sure all information can be verified
- Avoid using PO box numbers
- Provide a phone number & Skype handle
- Provide more than one way to contact you

  Give Yourself the Mom Test

  Would your mother approve of what you're saying on your website?

  Would your mom recognize your voice in your website content?

  Gather Recommendations from Industry Peers & Fellow Experts

  Make sure the endorsement is relevant to your audience

  Give A Gift

  Can be a free gift or a 'lite' version of your product

  Your gift should leave people wanting to do business with you

  Invest in Quality

  Every part of your business should project professionalism & quality

  Dig into Your Past for Expert Connections

  Many people are flattered that you remembered them & want their endorsement

  Show Photos on Your Website

  Helps people get to know you before they even meet you

  Offers proof to your potential customers

Network

Meet people in person at conferences, workshops, community events & mastermind retreats

Talk with the speakers, the emcee and the host

Be Positive

Come up with solutions for bad conditions

Show people how you handle pressure positively

Don't complain on social media

Dare to Share

Provide valuable information people can use immediately

Become a Published Author

Produce a top-quality, professional manuscript correctly formatted & thoroughly proofed

Please remember that you don't have to do backflips to establish your branded credibility. Just be professional, authentic and client focused.

Show Your AUTHORITY

Books have always been a guilty pleasure for me.

With every book I read, the power of what is printed on a single sheet of paper never ceases to amaze me. Whether it's a J.D. Robb who-done-it, a 'tongue in cheek' from Janet Evanovich, or business acumen from Michael Gerber, I am still left awed and inspired.

For hundreds of years, authors have been regarded with respect and admiration – Tolstoy, Nietzsche, Dickens. It's no wonder that today many entrepreneurs and speakers are published authors.

Do you see the major word that stands out when you see the word "authority?" AUTHOR! By becoming an author, one automatically claims their authority on the subject printed.

Being an author is the definitive demarcation line of attack, as it truly separates you from the pack.

Believe it or not, most authors do not write their books for the money. There really is very little money in books, unless you are a J.K. Rowling or a Donald Trump. In the real world of book writing, the actual purpose isn't the book. It's all about what the book will do for you. It's all about the new opportunities that will be created, as well as all the doors that will finally open for you.

Becoming a published author will afford you:

New-found respect and admiration

Personal satisfaction

Enhanced credibility

Expert status with your customers

New customer surge due to your increased credibility

Businesses, opportunities, and people naturally seek you

A high sense of accomplishment

Newfound connections and increased earnings

Credibility and esteem are what give authors an inside edge. This is an invaluable tool, which used properly, can translate into $$$.

When your customers trust their source, it makes it possible for them to make important decisions in their business.

The trust and authority granted to authors is already formed in the minds of the public. This knowledge is worth more than a king's ransom! This knowledge should be the foremost reason for becoming an author. It's all about the new opportunities, the previously closed doors opening, and the enhanced business relationships that being an author create. All this answers the question of:

"Why should I become a published author?"

Think about it. Would you rather work with an "Average Joe," or an "Author/Expert?" Of course you'd rather do business with the expert! So would the majority of the population. Writing a book will allow you to STAND OUT from your competition… and put you at the level of all the other leaders that you have admired.

The bottom line is that being an author automatically makes you a branded expert. If you want an enormous advantage over your competitors…then become a published author and brand yourself as the business expert in your niche.

There is no greater branding, or client enticement, than being a published author.

Whether you decide to write your own book, use a ghostwriter, or be included in a Multi-Author book with other leaders, there's no better way for you to create yourself as an authority. Once your potential customers realize that you are a published expert, they will be ready to work with you, while also referring you to others.

Being an author can multiply your chances of getting every customer you meet as a client. You'll profit from being an author for your entire life……

And no one can ever take that away from you.

Here's to taking the next step to becoming the published authority in your field!

C. Mike Lewis, *"The Book Guy"* has over 35 years of experience in marketing, finance, construction and real estate. He previously owned and operated several companies in the southeast, including a $100 million land development company.

He is the co-owner of Branded Expert Publishing, the top Ghost Publishing firm in the world, specializing in books, tools and resources for entrepreneurship and small businesses.

His products are practical, hands-on, and based on the real-world experiences of successful entrepreneurs, CEOs, investors, lenders, and seasoned business experts.

Mike's passion for turning non-writers into authors of printed books, with virtually no writing on their part, positively impacts and changes lives. Using his complete "Done For You" publishing service has helped raise his client-author's authority and recognition in all phases of their businesses.

mike@brandedexperts.com

404-281-6552

How To Live A Kapow Life
Bite Sized Lessons For Your Success

Liz Benny

Bite 1: Having Ideas Above Your Station

I'm from a small farm, at the bottom of New Zealand. Near Antarctica. I'm not kidding. It's cold down there. I was raised mostly by my father, and the farm dogs, and the chickens… as well as some help from my amazing grandparents.

As a young kid there was a general expectation that if you were sitting in front of the TV, you had ample time to help with chores around the farm. So "chores" was how I grew up. Chores like… picking up and sorting sheep poop off the shearing shed floor for 50c per hour.

Whilst doing these chores I'd dream… of all the inventions I could create that would help others. Like turning the green goop that gets stuck underneath a lawn mower into some really, really… green face mask sorta thing.

Anyway… I digress.

The point here is I dreamed and dreamed and dreamed as a kid…

And one day, as a much older 'kid' (I was 24) I was having a conversation with my grandmother about what I wanted to do with my life. I was so excited! I was telling her about my businesses I wanted to start and create.

Then in the heat of the excitement she said to me, "Elizabeth, do you have ideas above your station?" disapprovingly.

That confused me for a second…

And then I got it.

To her, I was thinking of a life above that which I was born into. To her, I wanted more than I was allocated.

See… I think to some degree we all have that person, or many people, in our family who think that way. And much of the time we entrepreneurs choose to stay small, to keep "in" with our family.

I'm glad I had ideas above my station. It helped me get to where I am now.

Make sure YOU have ideas above your station… and make sure you stay true to your path.

Bite 2: Living An Authentic And Kapow Life = True Success

Look, I'm just going to be honest with you. It's the only way.

For many, many, many years I hated myself. Genuinely hated myself. I told myself I could never be successful because of who I am.

"I'm disgusting"

"NO ONE will do business with me!"

"I"m just Liz Benny"

Now… I'm going to be **really** honest with you. It was not until I fully became OK with who I am that I started having success. I'm serious.

You see, I always knew that I'd end up spending my life with someone of the same gender. As hard as I tried… I couldn't change that reality. Believe me, I tried.

Now… I'm not doing to get into details… but please just listen to this (it'll save you a TON of pain)…

Once I started being my FULL SELF, almost like magic, I started having success in business.

Bite 3: Remember Where You Sleep

Being an entrepreneur can be wonderful! And… it can be lonely as hell.

The part I hate the most about being an entrepreneur is the rollercoaster. The ups… and the downs. The highs and the blows.

Many people have asked me, "What kept you going in all your lows Liz?"

And it was always, always my why. My family. They were my reason for keeping on going.

See I wanted to give up many times. Sometimes the blows came one after the other, so fast that I didn't know where the light was. Kristi, my wife, was hospitalised with a rare form of pneumonia and I thought at one stage I was going to lose her. She couldn't breathe properly.

At the same time we were homeless, living out of suitcases at a friend of a friend's house when they were on holiday. I literally created Social Monkey Business from the hospital beside AND from a stranger's house.

We'd been going backwards in our previous business, Jinga Social, because I wasn't taking on clients due to the time it was taking to get my webinar and training course off the ground.

I worked for months and months on end. Learning systems, learning how to put together marketing collateral, and doing the work I needed to do to be successful.

After a few months, I was ready to launch. No list, no "friends" online to promote me… just a little cash to get some folks on a live webinar using solo ads.

The first webinar I did, ever, was from a different friend's house… with the world's slowest internet connection.

Not one person showed up. I bawled my eyes out… and believe me… I wanted to throw in the towel. To me, I was going backwards at a rapid rate of knots… and as a perfectionist I didn't like that feeling at all. I would often think, "I might as well be working at the supermarket as a check-out chick rather than going through this"…

But I knew better. I knew there was other folks succeeding online… and if they could I could. I saw Amy Porterfield succeed. I saw Lewis Howes succeed. And to me the only difference between them and me was time (and skills they'd picked up along the way).

So, as hard as it was with all the blows… I kept going. For my family. I hated where we lived. I was ashamed of it. It was old, damp and it smelled bad. I knew it was up to me to keep going.

Here's the deal though. I didn't get where I am alone. SO… "Remember where you sleep" basically means that when you finally crack, when you finally breakthrough, when you finally succeed and make your first $20,000 month or $100,000 day… then remember where you came from. Remember those who supported you in your journey. THEY deserve that.

Say thank you, don't let money and success run your head, be humble and be so very grateful.

Bite 4: Don't Be A Freaking Squirrel!

An amazing thing happens when you start having "success". You start being "known" by people who you've looked up to for years and years. I've been friend requested by people who have been my heroes online … and it's completely blown me away.

That's a pretty cool deal, because it means you've done something awesome enough to get the attention of others. I'm not a big "ego" person… so when this type of stuff happens I take is as recognition of having made a difference in the world.

There are downsides to becoming… "known" too.

The bad side of being a successful entrepreneur is that, like moths to a flame, you'll start to be approached by every Tom, Dick and Harry wanting you to be a part of their next gig. You'll hear "what about this idea", or "Let's partner on this"… and before you know it… you could be swept up in project after project some of which you may not be the least bit interested in.

I've seen successful entrepreneurs lose out big time by doing this.

I'm the worst culprit. In 2015… after Social Monkey Business and my Coaching Platform were booming, I started another company that I had no business starting.

It was a great idea… but it was a train wreck. I'm being real with you here. That business cost me time and money (in set up fees and lost income) and… worse… it sent me to the doctors with stress pains in my chest. I literally could not breathe with the amount of "yucky" stressful feelings I was experiencing.

Don't be a squirrel. Period.

If you have a winning offer… stay CLOSE to that winning offer… And for goodness sake, listen to your gut. If your gut says "This deal/business idea is kinda not what I wanna do" But your head is saying "Oh this can make millions" … RUN as fast as you can. Seriously, run.

Now… there are other types of squirrels too… and you certainly don't wanna be one of those either.

These are the shiny object seekers. The "I'll try this for five minutes and if it doesn't work I'll do the next thing". I tried for YEARS and YEARS before I had success. With Social Monkey Business I fell flat on my face more times than I'd like to admit. But I kept going and found success.

Please just let the squirrels be squirrels. If you want success, focus on keeping the main thing the main thing. Adapt as needed (yes you can change the course slightly)… but don't change your businesses as often as you change your undies (this is the way New Zealanders say underwear).

Bite 5: What To Do When You Want To Give Up

Don't.

Just remember why you started.

Anchor that in… Remember your WHY.

Businesses that start with WHY are much, much, much more successful.

In all the times I wanted to give up, it was only my "why" that kept me going. Period.

Liz Benny is an entrepreneur and lifestyle coach who advocates that you live a 100% authentic life that you absolutely love through inspiration and action.

KNOWLEDGE IS THE NEW CURRENCY

ALICIA LYTTLE

The phone rang, it was August 17th, 2010 and I could see from the caller ID that it was Jennifer, my husband's assistant.

"Good Morning Jennifer, how are you?" I asked.

"Good morning Alicia. I have some news for you."

"Ok, what is it," I asked.

"You know that guys trip that your husband is going on? Well, he left his phone on the table, and I saw that he's not going with the guys, he's going with another woman. He's been having an affair and, it's been going on for a while."

"Thanks Jennifer, I'm going to call Lorette and get out of here while he's gone," I said.

The truth is, I was stuck in a very bad marriage for many years. I'd tried to get out before, but when I mentioned divorce he would go crazy on me. This was my chance to get out. I was actually happy he was having an affair, I was sure that when he found out that I found out, he would feel remorseful and be willing to let me go. I would later find out that I would be wrong on this assumption.

Anyway, when my sister arrived from Florida to help me out, we donated most my clothes and shoes to a woman's shelter. I packed up two suitcases, my laptop and my cell phone and left everything else. Then we started driving from my house in Texas to her apartment in Florida.

During the drive to her place, we stopped at the grocery store and I tried to use my debit card only to get a "declined' error at the checkout. Uh oh ....

Once we arrived at my sister's apartment, I opened up my laptop and logged into my accounts only to realize my greatest fear, I was now broke. I couldn't get into my email account, the passwords were changed on the database of over 400,000 people that we had and I couldn't even login to my domain and hosting accounts that contained the products my sister and I had created.

In an instant, everything we worked so hard to build in the past 10 years I was locked out of. We had a spreadsheet with the logins to all our accounts so that should something happen to any one of us, the others would be able to keep everything running. Well that excel sheet ended up being our enemy when it was in the hands of my now ex-husband.

That year our businesses had done the best ever. We had pulled in over 6 million dollars in the business, but at this moment I was broke. I went from being a millionaire, living in a 12,000 sq. foot mansion to sleeping on my little sister's sofa.

A few days after my family heard the news, my dad called and reminded me that I had a master's degree and could get a good government job. I politely replied back "Dad, I might not have any money in my bank account at this moment, but I am a millionaire."

As those words came out of my mouth, I believed them. I was a millionaire!

You see, I thought my ex-husband had taken away everything from me, the house, the money, my products, the client database, my personal and work email accounts …. but what I realized at this moment is that there is one thing that he could not take away, and that was my knowledge.

I knew how to build businesses and I could start over!

So we buckled down and my sister and I rebuilt from scratch fairly quickly. Now we have over 40 staff members, 3 offices and we have rebuilt a bigger business on our own terms.

What I learned on this journey was the power of knowledge. Knowledge is the new currency.

I was able to truly see the value of knowledge and understand that no matter where you are in life and what you face, if you have the knowledge, the drive and the discipline to succeed, you will be ok.

Now, my sister and I teach people all over the world how to leverage the power of the Internet for financial freedom. We give them the knowledge they need to start an online business. All you need is a start; continue to building upon that start and the sky is the limit for you.

Here are three things I want to leave you with:

1. Knowledge is the new currency. Learn, plan and take action on knowledge.
2. If you are starting online, start simple. I always recommend freelancing as a great place to start. Visit sites like fiverr.com and upwork.com and offer your skills and services on those sites.
3. Learn how to drive traffic. How will people see what you are offering? Nothing moves until you make a sale, and sales are made when people see your products and buy them! The fastest and easiest way to drive traffic is by using Social Media. Set up a Facebook page, an Instagram page, a YouTube channel, a Twitter account, and learn how to use them. You must pay for traffic, but you can start off by just spending $5 a day.

Our journey's in life takes us down paths that we might not understand, we might not think is "fair" or ask "why me", but when we look back on the rough times we see that they shape who we are and help us to create the value that we offer to the world.

I moved to Kingston, Jamaica a few years ago and I spend my free weekends sharing my knowledge with Jamaican's who want to listen. I teach them how to work online. In an economy where unemployment, especially among the youth is sky high and the minimum wage is $48USD a week, life is tough.

Just by working on their freelancing businesses, our students are making thousands of dollars a month, creating new opportunities for themselves, their families as well as teaching others how to work online. We teach them that knowledge is the new currency, and people are willing to pay for what you know.

Now, my mission is to change the economy of Jamaica by creating internet entrepreneurs who are earning from a global economy and spending their money locally to build the local economy. Can I do it? I'm one woman with a mission to change an entire country.

Of course I can do it. Watch me!

Alicia Lyttle is the CEO of Internet Income Jamaica, a training company that teaches people how to build an online business. She is also the CEO of Pow Social, The Caribbean's Leading Digital Marketing Agency.

Before jumping into entrepreneurship in the year 2000, Alicia had a career in Environmental Science and Policy. She has worked at some notable organizations, including The White House, The United States Environmental Protection Agency (USEPA), and The City of New Orleans in the Mayor's Office.

As a highly sought after speaker and trainer, Alicia has travelled around the world including Australia, the United Kingdom, New Zealand, Singapore, Malaysia, India, China, Japan, all over the Caribbean, Nigeria, South Africa, and many other countries, teaching and educating others on how to leverage the POWER of the Internet for financial freedom and business growth.

Alicia currently lives on the beautiful island of Jamaica.

5 Secrets to Continued Success

Matt Bacak

Develop these 5 attributes of a successful person, and you will find yourself moving quickly toward your goals in life!

- **Thick Skin**

You cannot be easily offended or hurt if you want to be successful. There will always be people who are jealous or envious or out to bring someone else down—you must develop a way to see past that and let it roll off your back, like "water off a duck's back."

Ducks have feathers that are tight and their density act like oil—it keeps the duck dry and warm. So when water (cold or otherwise) lands on the back of a duck, it simply rolls off. Let criticism roll off your back in a similar manner—because if you are going to be successful, you will have your share of criticism. Count on it.

- **Obedience:**

Although this might seem strange to talk about to adults and not children, it is important to consider that in order to be a leader, you must first learn how to obey a leader. You must learn the principle of loyalty to a leader if you want to lead others.

Once you have learned how to obey and to follow directions, you can lead others and understand what commands and orders do for an organization and an individual.

Consider this: 175 of the CEOs of Fortune 500 companies are former US Marines, and 27 US Presidents served in the military.

- **Courage:**

Bravery is not courage, but you cannot have courage without being brave. Courage is the moral fortitude to stand up for your character (touched on in the last article) and to do the right thing—even in the face of adversity.

When you have courage, you follow through on your vision. It's on display every day and only the courageous have the ability to get the most out of life. When you have the strength of your conviction, find the courage to put it in to action. You won't be sorry you did.

- **Intolerance:**

Not exactly what you might expect to find about success, but each of us must be intolerant of any number of things: intolerant of abuse, of injustice, of the things that you know are immoral, unethical, or illegal. If there's anything in this world you should be intolerant of, those are some of them. I hope you are an intolerant person—in the right way.

- **Sense of Humor:**

If you don't have a sense of humour, you will fall flat on your face and never be someone who succeeds. A good portion of the road we walk to success is filled with blockades and potholes. If you come up against one and go down, you must have the ability to laugh at the situation and yourself. If you don't, you will be angry and bitter about your misfortune and never move past it. Laugh at yourself and what you run up against and you'll find your climb to the top is quicker and more enjoyable than you thought it would be.

 **Matt Bacak** is considered by many an Internet Marketing Legend. Using his stealth marketing techniques, he became a Best Selling author with a huge fan base of over 1.2 million people in his niche as well as built multi-million dollar companies.

After being crowned, 2010 Internet Marketer of the Year, he was asked to appear on National Television, his Lifetime television segment focused on "how to make money using the Internet. The real way".

Matt is not only a sought-after internet marketer but has also marketed for some of the world's top experts whose reputations would shrivel if their followers ever found out someone else coached them on their online marketing strategies.

Made in the USA
San Bernardino, CA
05 April 2017